Life can be hard. Rachel has written a beautiful guide for living a full, rich, and abundant life even when it doesn't go how we'd like. As a woman who's walked through her fair share of unmet expectations, disappointments, and challenging circumstances, I recommend this to anyone struggling to make the most of the life they have—even if it doesn't look quite how you hoped it would.

JORDAN LEE DOOLEY, national bestselling author of *Own Your Everyday* and *Embrace Your Almost*

Rachel Awtrey is the girl who speaks to celebration—she helps us see that, even in hardship, we are able to find joy. This new book is an anthem for those of us struggling to see past our circumstances, reminding us that simple day-to-day changes can add up to a new, healthier perspective.

BOB GOFF, *New York Times* bestselling author, speaker, and coach

Love Your Life (Even When You Don't Like It All the Time) is the refreshing message we all need in a culture that lures us in with having it all, being it all, and killing it—all the time. You will come away feeling like you just sat with a best friend over coffee, having a hopeful change of perspective on your life, your mouth hurting from smiling so much, and filled with the strength to face your reality with true joy and gratitude. You will fall in love with Rachel, but even more so, you will see your life as a true gift even in the hard and mundane that you face daily.

ALYSSA JOY BETHKE, author of *When Doing It All Is Undoing You* and *Satisfied*

If you're craving an effortless and uplifting read, *Love Your Life* is for you. With honesty, witty humor, and spunk, Rachel not only urges us to claim the joy available in Jesus but gives us the practical tools to do so. Whether you're a wife, mom, entrepreneur, student, or empty nester, these pages hold truth for you.

TARA SUN, author of *Surrender Your Story* and host of the podcast *Truth Talks with Tara*

Rachel Awtrey's *Love Your Life (Even When You Don't Like It All the Time)* is a breath of fresh air. With warmth, honesty, and refreshing humor, Rachel invites readers to embrace the messy, mundane, and magnificent moments with a new perspective. This book isn't about pretending everything is perfect—it's about learning to find joy right where you are with God's transforming grace. Rachel's relatable storytelling makes *Love Your Life* feel like a heart-to-heart with a trusted friend, reminding us that even in the unexpected, there's beauty to be found. This isn't just a book; it's a companion for anyone seeking practical ways to cultivate joy and resilience. Rachel's wisdom expertly guided me to love my life more. Prepare to be inspired and changed by this must-read!

LARA CASEY ISAACSON, author of *Cultivate* and *Make It Happen*

Somewhere along the way we were convinced that a perfect life on this side of heaven was possible, and our fragile hearts were broken when we realized we'd have to fight for real joy. Thankfully, we've been gifted this beautiful book that Rachel has written to show us how to fight well. You can expect honest stories, practical rhythms, and finding magic in your very own life. What a gift.

TONI COLLIER, preacher, author of *Don't Try This Alone*, and podcast host

Rachel is a gifted writer, and through her relatability, storytelling, and truth, she makes you feel seen. Through her words, you feel like a friend is helping you not only to find joy in your life but also to blossom in whatever season you find yourself. I recommend this for everyone and anyone, but especially for young women in their twenties and thirties. Rachel will teach you how to embrace the life God has given you.

GRACE VALENTINE, bestselling author, podcast host, and speaker

The pages of this book felt like a gentle invitation. Rachel blends her heartfelt stories with practical advice, inviting you to settle into the joy that's already yours. I'm inspired to look inside the walls of my own home and to refresh my own rhythms rather than looking to "what's next" or "what's better" to find the life I love. The better is already mine for the taking, and Rachel showed me that.

NANCY RAY, host of the *Work and Play* podcast and mom of five

If you're tired of chasing joy and ready to simply embody it, this book is for you. Rachel's writing perfectly blends vulnerable storytelling with practical guidance, offering a hands-on approach to cultivating abundance in life's messy and hard moments. Rich with wisdom that's immediately actionable, this book had me furiously taking notes—and within hours, I was already revamping areas of my daily routine that were in desperate need of a joy upgrade. It's an empowering read for anyone ready to enter the "abundantly more" God invites us to experience daily with Him.

HANNAH BRENCHER, author of *The Unplugged Hours* and *Come Matter Here*

Relatable. Highly practical. Gracious. Deeply comforting. Life-giving. This book will meet you exactly where you are, especially if it's in a hard season or unexpected circumstance, and help you discover how to sing a different song over your life, with the help of the Holy Spirit. Rachel's words feel like a best friend sitting in your favorite comfy spot, offering you a warm cup and intently listening, while also having a bag full of maracas, soul-care items, and FUN to help you find your feet again. What a gift this book will be to those who need a true friend to help them fight for joy, recognize the fingerprints of God right where they are, and know that they are seen.

CLEERE CHERRY REAVES, bestselling author, podcaster, and owner of @cleerelystated

Reading this book felt like a breath of fresh air—a much-needed, cool drink of water for the soul. Rachel has a way of weaving together truth, courage, and storytelling that brings both tears and laughter, reminding us of the beauty found in both the brutal and beautiful parts of life. Her words don't just inspire; they invite, leading the reader to a deeper awareness of God's presence in everyday moments. This book is a treasure, one that lingers long after the last page is turned.

EMILIE McCORMACK, Breakaway Ministries

Rachel Awtrey serves up the REAL TALK we all so desperately need right now, with all the honesty, vulnerability, and practical advice of a trusted friend. The pages of *Love Your Life* are filled with Rachel's signature infectious joy and lighthearted humor, which she expertly uses to guide us—like a beacon in the dark—as we navigate into the more hard, holy, and heartbreaking parts of a life we might not LIKE very much right now. Reminding us that we could "wish our entire life away waiting for the next best thing" if we're not careful, Rachel instead points us to this powerful truth: life can be extremely difficult AND incredibly good—both can be true—but we can't fix what we won't get honest about. Rachel was BORN to write this book . . . and she can BOSS me around any time she wants! Read this *beautiful* book!

MARY MARANTZ, bestselling author of *Underestimated* and host of the *Mary Marantz Show*

love your life

(even when you don't like it all the time)

A REALISTIC GUIDE TO UNLOCKING JOY IN LIFE'S MESSY, MUNDANE & MAGNIFICENT MOMENTS

LOVE (even when you don't) YOUR (like it all the time) LIFE

RACHEL AWTREY

Tyndale House Publishers
Carol Stream, Illinois

Visit Tyndale online at tyndale.com.

Visit Tyndale Momentum online at tyndalemomentum.com.

Visit the author online at rachelawtrey.com.

Love Your Life (Even When You Don't Like It All the Time): A Realistic Guide to Unlocking Joy in Life's Messy, Mundane, and Magnificent Moments

Cover design by Libby Dykstra

Interior design by Cathy Miller

The author is represented by Alive Literary Agency, www.aliveliterary.com.

For manufacturing information regarding this product, please call 1-855-277-9400.

For information about special discounts for bulk purchases, please contact Tyndale House Publishers at csresponse@tyndale.com, or call 1-855-277-9400.

Library of Congress Cataloging-in-Publication Data

A catalog record for this book is available from the Library of Congress.

ISBN 979-8-4005-0513-3

Printed in the United States of America

31 30 29 28 27 26 25
7 6 5 4 3 2 1

To my dad, Bill, who left a trail of "legacy" joy.

CONTENTS

INTRODUCTION

My friends joke that I have a "black thumb," which is their kind way of saying plants come to my home to die. I'm guilty and will admit I'm that girl. Even though I know they won't last very long, I can't stop myself wanting to take my best shot at bringing home a spunky or colorful houseplant.

This time, it was an orchid.

Here's the thing I love about orchids: they are tall, stunning focal points for any room, which counts as decor in my book. As most plants do, this orchid came with a stake in the soil that listed care instructions so you "don't mess it up." In true Rachel fashion, I took that eyesore out as soon as I got home and tossed it in the garbage.

It's a plant. How hard can this be? All you have to do is water it!

Weeks went by, and I was the proudest I'd ever been when it came to my plant portfolio. I constantly sent update pictures to my friend group's message thread so they had evidence that I was, in fact, proving them wrong. I was redeeming my plant personality! I even gave my plant a name—Ophelia—to officially welcome her as a member of the family.

A few days later, Ophelia's petals started dropping. *Maybe she just needs more water?*

I carried the orchid to the sink, turned the faucet on, and let a stream soak the soil. As I took the orchid back to its home base, more petals kept falling off. Thirty-six hours later, every last bloom was gone. I was staring at a naked green twig with floppy leaves.

If I had kept the stake and read the information, I would have known that orchids actually don't need to be watered every day. A dip in the water so the bottom roots can drink once a week is enough for a thriving orchid. Because of my overwatering, the roots had rotted. Although there was a chance that Ophelia could be revived, the odds were slim. I'd have to take her out of her pot, cut the rotten roots off, and repot her in a container with a little bit more space to grow. And, obviously, I'd have to stop watering her so much.

I was doing my best to treat the symptoms of what I thought was a thirsty plant. But if I had known what to do, Ophelia would still be blooming.

Much like me.

Following the world's directions to loving our lives can be a lot like continuing to water an overhydrated plant.

When I "don't like life," I'm tempted to buy the newest trendy accessory, attempt a new recipe, make a new friend, binge a new series, book a vacation or staycation, or—heaven forbid—buy a new houseplant. I've been taught to treat my symptoms and try my best to get things right, to make myself happy and pull myself up by the laces of my favorite pair of sneakers (I'm not so much for bootstraps).

But more often than not, that's not what's needed. More often than not, I'm only adding to the problem.

How do we stop the madness? Hindsight, they say, is twenty-twenty: if I had called some of my gardening friends before things got so dire for Ophelia, the diagnosis might not have been terminal. After all, there were signs that something was up and Ophelia was starting to die. The leaves were wilted instead of firm, the stem became a bit more droopy, and the blooms weren't so perky anymore. All of this happened before the petals fell off.

Can we train ourselves to notice the wilting leaves, the droopy stem, and the blooms that are no longer thriving? Can we slow down long enough to get curious instead of charging forward as we always have?

I'm not just talking about houseplants, of course.

Part of liking your life is admitting that, sometimes, you don't. We can't fix what we won't get honest about. If today was challenging, frustrating, or chaotic, let's call it what it is. Because if the reason for the bad day stays hidden, tomorrow may look very similar. And sometimes it feels really embarrassing to admit that the typical things are piling up, and even though you're trying so hard to keep things alive, your petals . . . well, they're starting to droop. It doesn't mean you're not capable or resilient or that you can't have a green thumb when it comes to life.

Really, it's the first step toward blooming.

PART ONE

unlocking joy

the keys you didn't know you had

CHAPTER 1

WHAT IS JOY? (BECAUSE THE DICTIONARIES GOT IT WRONG AND WE MAY HAVE TOO)

Anxiety does not empty tomorrow of its sorrows, but only empties today of its strength.

CHARLES SPURGEON

My husband, Thomas, is a pilot—and he's out of town again. His flight was delayed by weather or some maintenance issue—I'm not sure, and I wasn't able to stay on the phone long enough or hear him over the whines and cries of my two toddlers fighting in the background. One of them got sick earlier this week, and yesterday someone shared the other's milk, and now—oh, look! They're both sick.

You can do this, Rachel. You just have to keep on keeping on.

You've got to be kidding me right now.

I cannot catch a break.

Bless it. Of course this would happen to me.

Ugh.

My day has been so busy keeping them occupied and off one another, administering medicine, and offering snuggles that my hands haven't stayed empty enough to throw that load of laundry into the washer. And if I did want to put a new basket of clothes in the wash, that would mean rerunning the cycle of laundry I forgot about, which is now spoiled and needs another rinse. A quick SOS call to my sister-in-law Lauren will help. Then I can get dinner on the table, and maybe I can call my neighbor Katy to see if we could pop over for a change of scenery—oh, wait, I can't bring sick kids to someone else's house. Never mind.

Don't dwell—put on a happy face. Your life is better than so many others'.

This is just a season—no need to feel sad. It's not going to change anything.

But before I know it, the molehills turn into mountains. I trip over one too many Hot Wheels scattered across the floor. One too many flight delays force me to be flexible, one too many external factors outside of my control demand I "go with the flow," something I imagine all the cool moms on Instagram can do effortlessly—but for me it feels like being dropped into another country without speaking the language.

In my head, I knew it was just a bad day.

So why, in my heart, did it feel like a bad life?

So Hard, but So Good

I'll be honest that this—admitting that sometimes I don't like my very likable life—isn't a place I want to go. I want to be the happy girl who doesn't constantly complain, who can be spontaneous and quirky and laugh at jokes and let her kids play in the dirt and not freak out, and who embraces the present for what it is instead of what it could be.

Sometimes I am that girl. I can throw a party like no one else; I can revel in my kids running wild in the backyard. But I told myself that if I ever put pen to paper, I would try to be honest even when it hurts.

And honestly, sometimes I'm the other girl too.

It's the reason I cried yesterday and the conversation that will probably come up again next week when my girlfriends ask how I'm doing: even though everything looks good on paper, even though I've worked really hard to build a beautiful, shiny life . . . there are days that still feel a little lackluster.

Can we all give each other permission to stop hiding and admit that both girls can coexist? We can absolutely be grateful for the life that God has given us—and sometimes we can have days or months or years where, even in that gratitude, we wish things were a little different.

Maybe you've seen the overflowing sink of dishes, the muddy paw prints on the freshly cleaned couch, the toddler who knocked over the pile of laundry you just folded, the Wi-Fi that goes out right when you're trying to finish that work project. You've thought, *Things should be better than they are,* only to realize you're wishing your life away by waiting for the next best thing.

Or maybe it's not the little things getting you down—it's the whole season you find yourself in. *Rachel, I WISH I were only dealing with a plethora of Hot Wheels to trip over.* Maybe you're bearing weighty circumstances that you can't see the end of. Caring for a medically fragile child. Struggling to catch your breath in the throes of postpartum. Wandering through the wilderness of a dry spell in your relationship with God. These seasons aren't solvable today, but they're supposed to be solvable someday, right? Right?!

Even worse, maybe your world has been rocked by larger, earth-shattering moments you never would've chosen—yet still have to live through.

I've been there. I *am* there. But here is what I've learned, here is what I know for sure: life is so hard, but it's so good. I know—even though we've never met—that your life is worth liking, even on your worst days. I know it because that's how God designed it—how He designed you.

He designed all of us to see the need for something far bigger and better than what is currently sitting in front of us and in our way of experiencing joy. Both can be true: life can be extremely difficult and incredibly good.

It can be broken and beautiful.

It can be strained and strategic.

It can be hard and holy.

So What Is Joy, Anyway?

If you're in a spot where your days are lackluster, if you're in a spot where you want to like what you have but don't, let's get real about it.

I think about all of the times that I'm asked quickly in passing, "How are you?" and I respond, "Great!" There is a time and a place, and the frozen pizza aisle at the grocery store is not always the time to go into why life feels off. But when we carry this habit into rooms and conversations where the honesty does belong, I wonder how often we'll miss out on being fully known because who we pretend to be is not who we really are in that moment.

You don't need to "cheer up, buttercup."

You don't need to "have an attitude of gratitude."

You don't need to "just look on the bright side."

This is not a book to "bibbidi-bobbidi-boo" fix your problems. We have enough of those voices in our own heads. It's also not a book to tell you the opposite, that liking your life is one fancy gadget or affiliate link away—that in three easy steps, you can build a self-reliant life where you don't need Jesus.

This is a book to teach you how to fight for joy. It can be really hard to like your life sometimes. It's not just going to happen. You have to work for it. I don't want things to get in the way of seeing and then living lives that are abundant and beautiful. But the people who like their lives are the people who are willing to fight.

And your life is worth fighting for.

But before we can fight for a joy-filled life, we've got to understand what joy is . . . and what it's not.

Maybe we've had the concept of joy all backward?

I'll go first: I thought joy was in a destination. But it's in the journey.

I thought joy was a gift to earn once I "got through something." But it's available right now.

I thought joy was what I had to look forward to. But it's in the mundane right in front of us.

I thought joy was feeling happy all the time. But there is a very distinct difference between joy and happiness, even though many people assume they mean the same thing.

Happiness is the feeling you have based on what's happening *around* you.

Joy is the feeling you have based on what's happening *inside* you.

It's not dependent on your circumstances, relationships, or other emotions, and it can exist when everything else feels like it's falling apart. Joy is not toxic positivity. It's nodding to the issues around you without bowing to them.

Want to know one of the best things about joy? Joy can be found wherever you look for it. Happiness can't.

When you start to look for it, you can't help but notice it . . .

. . . everywhere.

The way the morning light comes through your window and makes floating dust motes look like glitter.

The way the smile lines crease the sides of your eyes from so many grinning moments.

The way the sky turns pink before it turns blue if you catch it at the right time of sunrise or sunset.

The way a "Hey, I'm thinking about you" text can make all the difference in our day.

I could go on.

How kind of God to give us these detailed gifts to bring us joy. He is at work in our lives, going to great lengths to bring us back to Him. Let's make room to see it.

When I have conversations like this with dear friends in my life who trust me to help them hold their realities, this is about the point where they start tapping out. They think pursuing joy in their everyday lives is too idealistic, assume that I truly have no idea what they're walking through. But let's pretend you and I are at that table, face-to-face. I'd grip your hands like I grip theirs and tell you a truth that changed my life: we can't have good news if we don't have bad news. It's quite difficult to enjoy a peak without hiking the hill. If we've never experienced heartbreak or hopelessness, then healing and hope are easily casualized instead of marveled over for what they actually are. There's nothing to celebrate if there's nothing to groan over: childbirth and birthdays to come, the process and the product, the fight to run the race and the triumphant finish. It's a both/and.

So many of us find ourselves overwhelmed and buried in what we are facing right here, right now. We become so tunnel-visioned that we miss what God is doing to our left and our right.

Let me ask you this: Can you see where God is showing up for you today? No shame if you can't. It may even be painful to lean in and mentally be where you are because it's just not where you want to be. Please don't believe the fairy tale that putting blinders on to get the job done will help you through life. Being present is where we see His presence.

There's Enough Room

Maybe we've avoided talking about joy and having that as our baseline because it seems tone-deaf in a world that often seems like it's falling apart. "Life is life-ing" is the typical 911 text I send to my friends when I feel constantly hit by waves and finally get my head above water high enough to call out for help.

I joke with our neighbors that when life just gets too stinking hard and we need a break, we'll set off our car alarms as a cry for help.

For the longest time, I misunderstood joy—I would have viewed these "car-alarm" moments as episodes that joy could never be part of. But now that I have an accurate idea of what joy is, I've realized it's present in these moments too. Maybe that's where the world has gotten it wrong all along: joy and chaos, pain, grief, and hardship can, and do, coexist.

Life is actually really hard.

We must stop believing that life has to be easy before we experience a life of abundance.

We must stop believing that it's one or the other: fullness of joy or fullness of grief.

We must stop believing that we must choose between healing and facing reality.

The enemy of joy is not grief or hardship or suffering. Grief, hardship, suffering, sadness, and anger all have a place. There's enough room at the table for all these feelings. Experiencing joy does not mean that your hardships or "car-alarm" moments are any less real; it just makes them lighter, briefer, more purposeful.

The enemy of joy is the enemy of our souls and the enemy of us living "our best life"—the life God intends us to have with Him.

The tension is where we see our need for resources beyond our own. God is kind to weave Himself in and through every detail that we could delight in and depend on Him for.

Because let's be real for a second: if life were comfortable, would we see the epic need for a Comforter?

If we could solve all our problems on our own, would we be quick to pray? Would we raise our eyes and marvel at all the ways God sees us through and sits with us in the midst of hard things? Or would we hurry to take the credit and pat ourselves on the back?

I have a feeling if my life were beautiful without being broken, strategic without moments of strain, and holy without anything hard, it would be a challenge to lean in and see my great need for a relationship with the Lord.

God has designed us and everything else in creation to ache for Him and eventually be renewed by Him. And because He's an incredible Father, He gives us beautiful, joyful lives in the midst of the brokenness on earth. He gives us strategic relationships even when other relationships are strained, and He gives us holy hope when life gets hard. As the psalmist says of God, "You make known to me the path of life; in your presence there is fullness of joy; at your right hand are pleasures forevermore" (Psalm 16:11). We have access to the fullness of joy, and God has pleasures in store for our lives.

But here is what I also know: the enemy wants us to live a subpar, mediocre, almost-but-not-quite kind of life. He wants us to feel stuck in the could'ves and should'ves. He wants the past to haunt us and the grief to overwhelm us and act like a bungee cord attaching our hearts to the hurt. Just as much as God wants us to experience the joy of life around us, the enemy wants to keep us distracted—too confused and fatigued to pursue joy. Because when we agree that rough moments and seasons get the final say, the enemy wins. The opposer to our abundant, beautiful, God-wink-filled lives smirks, knowing that we won't experience the fullness of who God is.

I have good news for you: it doesn't matter where you've been, what you've done, who you are, or who you're not—you aren't disqualified from loving your life. This isn't me dismissing you or what you're going through. The opposite, my friend. I see you. There's a reason you're in the place you find yourself, and I hold space for that. You get every permission to feel the way you feel, and I agree that yes, this life can be really hard.

But I also want to give you hope. If we can follow the trail of annoyances, irritations, transitions, heaviness, and barriers to contentment—well, my friends, then we'll know what it takes for long-lasting joy to be ours.

Good Means Abundant

This is different than I expected.

This is really tough.

These are thoughts I have on a regular basis. My imagination is pretty lively, and I think up a lot of best-case scenarios. When reality doesn't quite live up to what I pictured, I find myself a little twitchy. I've talked with enough friends to know it's not just a "me" thing. Frustration is just a missed expectation. When life lets me down, I find myself frustrated.

When my date night with Thomas doesn't go the way I planned, I'm bothered and discontented. No matter if our meal was amazing, our conversation was fruitful, and we got ice cream at the end.

When the park day turns into a chaotic adventure and doesn't meet my "I'm a cool mom" aspirations, I feel defeated. No matter if my kids left sweaty and happy, we ran into friends at the playground, or we stopped for a fun treat.

But what about the frustrating moments that feel a bit heavier?

When we found ourselves struggling to pay rent in the early days of marriage, and it left us without the budget to do anything fun, I felt unsettled.

When it took us longer to get pregnant than we thought it would, I felt discouraged.

When the military has us move *again*—sooner than we anticipated—and I find myself hovering over cardboard boxes, wrapping up our items once more, I feel disappointed.

In those fragile and frustrating times, it's easy for me to believe that it "shouldn't be this difficult," and therefore something's wrong with me or wrong with where I am.

It's also easy for me to assume that because life is tough or different than it ought to be, it's bad. This mindset steers me away from all the beauty that can be found within the pivots.

In moments like those, I'm tempted to "just get through it" to the other side. But when I'm so focused on getting through, how much do I miss in my peripheral vision by hoping joy will be easy to find once I'm out of this season I didn't sign up for?

Perhaps the grass isn't greener on the other side. Perhaps it's actually greener when I choose to water it where I'm standing.

A "good" life doesn't mean a life that's comfortable, easy, or free of obstacles. A "good" life is an abundant life (see John 10:10). And an abundant life is one that's full: full of the joy God provides.

Here's the secret to finding a joyful, abundant life worth celebrating even when you didn't sign up for the one you're living. Remember that both can be true: life can be really hard, but it can also be really good.

Grab the Grocery Cart, Please

"We just need detergent and creamer!" Thomas said as I rounded the corner, grabbed the car keys, and headed out the front door. It was one of those grocery trips that maybe we could get by without, but it would be nice to do the laundry that night and have creamer in our coffee the next morning.

"Detergent and creamer. Detergent and creamer," I reminded myself. Not that I was worried I'd forget—I was trying to keep myself from adding to the list. You probably know this well: you go into a store for one thing but leave with several additional items. In our defense, sometimes we don't know we need something until we see it, right? That vibrant bouquet of flowers would look perfect on your table. That treat would be a fun surprise for your child. And a friend just had a baby, so a pick-me-up from the bakery would be a sweet gesture. Then there's the yogurt on sale, the peanut butter you remembered you're out of, and the gum near the checkout. Before you realize it, your arms are full, and now you regret not grabbing a grocery cart when you first walked through the doors.

"You've got your hands full!" exclaims the grocery store clerk.

"Sure do!"

"Should've grabbed a grocery cart."

"Sure should have!"

How did detergent and creamer turn into this? Do I really need it all?

I really wish I could say grabbing more than I originally needed and trying to make it without dropping anything doesn't happen that often, but I confess it does. I'll go a little further and say that this experience goes beyond the grocery store.

It happens in the way I manage my time: *I can pull that off this afternoon.*

It happens with the way I take on responsibilities: *I'm sure I can fit that in. It's just once a week.*

It happens with the way I view life. *If I can just make it through this season, I'll be okay.*

Before I know it, my arms are full (and not in a good way).

We're all carrying things, whether it's a job, a family, a dream, grief, difficulties, celebrations, expectations, fill in the blank. Some of these are light, some heavy, some clunky. And that's life: picking up, dropping off, switching arms. Isn't it?

Maybe freedom from these things doesn't come from carrying them differently or solving the world's biggest problems or learning how to cope and numb ourselves. Maybe freedom comes from putting them down.

I'm not suggesting you become irresponsible and neglect what's yours to hold. But if you're used to juggling it all, I have an idea for you. What if the freedom we keep talking about doesn't look like solved problems but like supporting everything with something other than your own two arms?

Somewhere along the way, we started believing that muscling through our hardest days by carrying the weight ourselves was a badge of honor. We believed it would make us stronger, more intelligent, more inspiring to the people around us. The idea of "vulnerability" turned into this ideal of sharing all the clunkiness in our life while the idea of actually enjoying something became "fake." But we're not any more mature or wise because we skipped out on the fun.

Grocery stores have carts for a reason, after all: to carry everything for us, to take it from aisle to aisle, to disperse the weight and make it all a bit lighter.

That's joy.

It's a gift from God that allows us to see life as fun and enjoy what's around us even though we're pushing heavy things.

It creates more margin to focus on the tasks at hand.

It gives us levity to survive our hardest days.

For the things you don't have a choice whether to carry (like your child's chronic illness, a messy divorce, grief over the loved one you lost, the heartache that lingers after harsh words were said), may I suggest you place them in the cart? Jesus invites us to set these things down and trust His mechanics over our ability to muscle through: "Come to me, all who labor and are heavy laden, and I will give you rest" (Matthew 11:28).

So not only is joy *available* to us, but it's also an invitation.

My prayer for you is that joy becomes so natural, so easy, so habitual that it is just something you do. I pray that you won't know any other way to grocery shop than to push a cart and set all your items inside.

No, Really—You Can Do This

If you lean in and take a chance on this idea of finding joy in the middle of a life you don't always like, you will walk away from this book a different person—for the sake of yourself, your home, your community, and the Kingdom.

There are a lot of glorious guides, like self-help books and personal development strategies, to help us identify how we feel and what we feel and what to do with those feelings, but I thrive on the practicals—the road maps and to-do lists, the scripts for conversation and "just tell me how" answers to my questions. That's what I want to give you.

We'll start by looking at how we approach life—because that's going to have everything to do with how we feel about our day-to-day. You may be constantly tripped by hurts and hang-ups that are just plain annoying. You may be working through a tough season that you can't see the end of. You may be walking through a tragedy, and life feels fragile. As much as I wish it were true (because, heck, things would be a whole lot easier), there is no one-size-fits-all approach to how we walk through life, deal with difficulties, or find ways to pursue joy through it all. So we've got to do a pulse check, find the heartbeat and rhythm of our current life, and determine the appropriate next steps to take with grace.

I get it—the idea of looking at life squarely and being honest with where we are can be daunting. I promise to make it fun, and I'll always share first. That's what friends are for.

After that, we'll get down to the practical: how we can actively pursue joy in the day-to-day through our rhythms, our friendships, our homes, and more. Once we've established these patterns of joyful living, we won't be quite so whiplashed when things fall apart.

Just as much as I want you to like your life (love it, even) and live in abundance that other people can't help but notice, God wants that for you way more. Take your time. Take what you need. Ask God to show up majorly in your life through the reading of this book, and start an account of where you notice Him moving. Because He is.

Imagine the best version of you that still has laundry piling up, still trips on a Hot Wheels toy, still has the person who's hard to love in your life, still has the responsibilities you have to carry, but . . .

You feel more vibrant.

You notice the beauty around you.

You see the margin to include others.

You have the space to brush off silly things that once tripped you up.

You have the mental bandwidth to have conversations without being depleted.

You see the opportunities for play.

You turn to prayer before anything else.
You find joy when you surrender.
This is for you. This is so possible.

CHAPTER 2

THAT WASN'T ON MY BINGO CARD

Rejoice in hope, be patient in tribulation,
be constant in prayer.

ROMANS 12:12

I couldn't catch my breath. My ears were ringing. The sheets on the bed all of a sudden felt scratchy, and the news I'd just received was too impossible to be real. My stomach tightened, and immediately the blood left my toes. I tried to absorb the words that my mom had just spoken over the phone.

"Cardiac arrest. Do you guys know what that means?"

Theoretically, yes. In real life, no.

It wasn't uncommon for Dad to do something exhilarating and borderline chaotic. It was the least he could do after being sick for so long. Learning Arabic, doing business overseas, sharing the gospel unapologetically, competing in triathlons, driving race cars—full-on "Live Like You Were Dying" Tim McGraw kind of stuff.

By the time I was eight, my little brain had known a lot of trauma: car accidents, a dad on dialysis, surgeries for little brothers. Thankfully, I was in therapy, and a professional helped me wrangle my heart to accept the reality that Dad wouldn't live forever. Because of kidney failure, years of dialysis now failed, and a long transplant list, I had come to terms (as much as possible for a second grader) that this was what life was like—dangerous and unpredictable, which in return required much caution from me.

"Relief" doesn't even begin to explain the feeling I experienced when I could finally say the therapist was wrong—Dad *was* going to get better thanks to Mrs. Judy, a woman who was a stranger at the time. Mrs. Judy was a member of our church who was moved to start the donor process and see if she'd be a match. Sure enough, she was the perfect match. She became one of my heroes when she donated her own kidney to replace my dad's so that he could live until he was old and gray (at least, that's what should have happened).

Jesus met me in a cold—but somehow also warm—hospital room swirling with hope after my dad's successful transplant. Dad's frail, fair-skinned body looked more alive than he had in years. That day, he shared something with me that I'll never forget. It changed my heart forever.

I like to think that my dad was able to exhale, physically and spiritually, and his breath breathed a new revelation into me. This moment—just the two of us in his hospital room shortly after his successful surgery—turned into a landmark moment for me. I sat in the guest recliner in the hospital room, eating orange sherbet and kicking my legs to the beat of the beeping machines. Out of nowhere my dad took an uncomfortable breath, readjusted himself a little, and with a croak in his voice spoke Truth over me. "Just like Mrs. Judy gave me her kidney so I could live my life abundantly instead of in bed, sick all day, Jesus gave His life for you so you could live a full life without your heart being sick anymore."

I continued eating the sherbet. His words were so clear to me: I didn't have any follow-up questions, head tilts, or anything. It was something I had heard all my life growing up in Sunday school, singing children's songs, and listening in "grown-up church." But for some reason, that day it clicked. It made sense . . .

. . . until fast-forward eight years later when I found myself back in a hospital room with my mom and brothers, holding my dad's pillow tight with white knuckles, hearing "He's home with Jesus." Suddenly, I didn't know anything anymore. My brain bent in ways I'm still chasing healing for.

Here's what had happened: "It's another day for adventure," Dad said early that morning as he collected his gear, packed the car, picked up a friend, and drove to the mountains of Asheville, North Carolina. I had an orthodontist appointment that morning to get my braces removed, and we were planning to celebrate with a big dinner that evening.

The call would come later that afternoon, after my appointment. We learned that Dad had fallen while rock climbing. He had been helivaced to a hospital.

I never imagined he wouldn't be coming home.

I couldn't tell if this was the beginning of my worst nightmare or the end of the best life I would ever know.

I was sixteen: bulletproof and brave. That girl, in an instant, melted into a wreck in her parents' bedroom. My worst fear had materialized into reality in a matter of minutes.

Adventure took away my dad—the transplant survivor, the invincible man, full of joy and zeal. The smile lines around his eyes, the cheesiest of grins, and the truth of everything I knew vanished with him. Everything I thought I knew about God was called into question too.

If God is good, then why?

Does God really listen to me, or does He just hear me?

Mind-altering thoughts began to take shape—and then started shaping me.

My life will never be the same. How will I ever laugh again? I'll feel like this forever.

And most importantly—*Will I ever get a break from the sorrow?*

This one. This one haunted me.

Maybe it was because a cackle over a dumb joke was something so common for me that my friend group made fun of my laugh. When we drove around town, I loved to break out in dance with the music loud and the windows down. Every week, I could be found under our high school's Friday night lights watching whatever sport was in season, and every Sunday afternoon I had the time of my life at youth group. My personality type was "I'll give it a try," so I did it all: student council, gospel choir, golf, track and field—anything that made life more active, social, and fun.

But all of a sudden I didn't feel permission to live that life anymore. I mean, how could I? Everything I knew, everything I wanted, everything my mind had ever imagined about my future was no longer possible—at least, that's what I thought.

I wish I knew then what I know now: what you feed is what will grow.

That version of Rachel was feeding her own misery through toxic behavior, doing anything to just "get rid of it" to "find myself." If I'm allowed to be painfully honest with you, it's what I thought I was *supposed* to do as I grieved. Some people in my life seemed to almost encourage this behavior.

I grossly misinterpreted recommendations to "Take the time you need" and "Do what you need to do to feel better," which kept me stuck longer than I ever should have been. The majority of my conversations at that time revolved around the expectation that I would be sad. I suppose I was given too much grace, compassion, sympathy, and time to ruminate. Many people painted despair on me and gave me every excuse to sit in the unlocked cell I found myself in. I agreed with it all and convinced myself I was trapped. I was shocked at how quickly my life could change, that my dad's dirty laundry was still in the hamper and receipts from his gas station stop forty-eight hours before still sat on his nightstand. There's no rule book or go-to guide on how to grieve. There's no barometer to tell you if you're doing it well or creating collateral damage through it all. I found myself using people's gestures as opportunities to escape reality and avoid responsibilities. They were the bumper rails to my bowling lane of life. Who was I to enjoy my life?

My friends were gracious enough to throw me a birthday party that year. It's important to note here that my dad died only a few days before I turned seventeen, so my friends had to plan it around all the mournful gatherings of the week: visitation on Tuesday, birthday on Wednesday, and then pack up the party and morph into funeral mode for Thursday. Everything felt off-balance.

A few hundred high schoolers—it felt like everyone I'd ever passed in a hallway—showed up in my backyard on that cold January night. They did it all: gifts, a good playlist, and a cake. I'd even gone out with my girlfriends that morning to buy a new outfit for the party—and for the funeral.

You know birthday parties: hugs, dancing, laughter—everything that "isn't allowed" a few days after your dad dies. That's written in some rule book somewhere, right? *There's no room for happiness and joy anywhere in these dark places,* I thought. *I'll have to wait until life feels normal again—if it ever does.*

I actually believed this for years. Too many years. The next four years, the "after" years, were overflowing with joy, growth, goodness, reconciliation, friendship, broadening of dreams, and so much more. But I shut them down and shut them out. I grieved hard. I grieved messily. I grieved ugly. That was the only narrative I knew.

In hindsight, the evidence of a good life was there. Helpful conversations happened, solid mentors were in place—I just wanted nothing to do with them. I signed on some dotted line somewhere, agreeing to an oath that a lot of us have put our names to at one point or another. I believed that joy could not exist where despair was present.

I was wrong. I was so wrong.

If you knew me the last few years of high school and into college, you probably knew a different version of me than I am now. I was innately the rebellious girl who had to touch the stove to know it was hot. I thought my family's tragedy gave me permission to be that girl, to try everything I'd ever been curious about.

Here's the thing—I'm still rebellious, and I think that's one of God's favorite things about me. But now I'm rebellious in a different way. It took people who knew me and loved me and called out the best in me to shepherd this behavior into a direction of life rather than destruction. I found freedom from the defiance through other people standing firm in the midst of my fragility. Someone in my sorority also gifted me a sign painted with 2 Corinthians 3:17: "Now the Lord is the Spirit, and where the Spirit of the Lord is, there is freedom." I hung it on the back of my door, and it nudged me in the direction of grace and true freedom. Instead of challenging boundaries, rules, and authority, I began challenging the despair I couldn't shake in my darkest days. Now I rebel against the thought that life has to be one or the other: good or hard.

This is for you if you've had the thought *You don't know my story* or *You don't know my hurt.* I don't. But I do know a God who's big enough to help us with our hurts and hang-ups, and I know the joy He has in store for us every morning.

Let me remind you of this: pain does not disqualify you from experiencing joy. In fact, it can be the motivation to jump all in and find joy. It's sitting right in front of you.

The enemy wants us to live a subpar, mediocre, almost-but-not-quite kind of life. He wants to keep me in a corner on days I accidentally call my dad's number and no one answers. He wants you to feel stuck in the could'ves and should'ves. He wants the past to haunt you and the grief to overwhelm you. If Satan can keep you hiding from God because of your hurt or bitterness toward Him, you won't experience the fullness of who God is.

God has given you only one shot at life.

Who told you that you can't experience joy in the middle of the hard? Why can't it be both: joyful and painful?

The question isn't "Which one should I feel?" The question is "Am I going to allow myself to feel joy in the midst of this pain?"

Impractical, you might be thinking. Can you trust me when I say it's not?

I've realized the most rebellious thing I can do is swim against the current of life and choose a different system. Joy goes against all the world's narratives: *How can I see that on the news and still find joy? How can I embrace joy even though I don't love this stage of my life?* To live in joy is to rebel against what's always been, or what will be true for you, despite how you'd want to see it happen.

So how do we hold both? I'm so glad to take you on that adventure.

Joy Holds It All Together

I want to remind us both of a truth I easily forget: we are not immune to suffering. It will happen to everyone. But sometimes we get tangled up in the belief that being a Christian means we should be exempt from hard days. It makes a lot of sense that we feel confused when grief and suffering come our way if "it wasn't supposed to be like that."

Here's the truth: hard times will come—we just have to access truth and hope when we're going through them. God has given us a trail to find joy even when things are unraveling. We're not immune to suffering, but we're not immune to joy in the middle of it, either. As the apostle Paul writes in Romans 8:18, "I consider that the sufferings of this present time are not worth comparing with the glory that is to be revealed to us." We're not told to write off the hardships of the human experience. In fact, Paul experienced suffering to a degree I doubt many of us ever have or will. So isn't it interesting that Paul himself considers the future, heavenly hope far better than the mess that today brings? Loving your life comes from knowing, accepting, and moving to a place that believes good days and bad days can work together to make a life we love.

My two little boys delight in picking me flowers. Some are full flowers pulled from my potted plants, which I grin at and tell myself will grow right back. Others are borderline weeds that were picked from a neighbor's yard. But most of the time, more than one petal has been tugged off by their curious little hands that don't understand the fragility of the flower quite yet.

Although the petals have been plucked, the middle (pistil) stays intact. In fact, it's impossible for the petals to grow there without the pistil but quite possible for the pistil to be present without the petals.

Like the petals of a flower, our life is made up of different facets, feelings, and friendships that could easily be bent, broken, or removed completely. But the joy, the rebellious gift to see life as beautiful, even with all our petals missing, can still be present.

To go one step further—just as the petals have no chance of sticking to a stem without the pistil, our life has no chance of being lovely without the centerpoint of joy.

If joy is the middle of the flower, it holds all the petals together. If the petals are important elements of our lives, the pieces that make our lives what they are, we can't guarantee they'll stay connected to the middle of the flower forever. And if your life played out anything like mine after losing my dad, most of the petals will fall off—one by one—until all you're left holding is the innermost part of the flower.

All my ideas could float away, my future could look different than I imagined, people could walk out of my life and make decisions I wouldn't have dreamed they'd make. But I can still be left with joy. It is still possible to see it, have it, and use it—it just doesn't look like the flower I thought it would be.

Here's the thing about a pistil: botanists would tell you that it contains more seeds for other flowers, and its main function is to produce a seed-bearing fruit. Not only can you hold on to joy as the middle of your flower no matter how many petals fall off, but you have the potential to grow again, to use what's left to start new, to bear fruit. I wish I could go back to the version of Rachel who watched her life fall apart after her dad's death. I would tell her so many things. I'd beg her to plant the pistil.

Planting the pistil means fighting for new friendship when you feel betrayed by the one you knew best. It means having the brave conversation that may take away comfort but give you a peace that surpasses understanding. It means honoring the dream you lost by championing others and cheering them on instead of harboring resentment.

And the blossoms that come after doing the hard work . . . breathtaking.

Joy Yields a Life You Love

Joy is a fruit of the Spirit, and if we know anything about the way fruit grows, we know it must be tended to. The soil must be tilled, the weeds must be plucked, the roots must be watered, and the fruit must be harvested once it has reached its prime. We must find ways to harvest joy in our own life too.

Maybe the idea of enjoying your life, being content with it, and finding ways to delight in the details has gotten a bad rap because it seems frivolous. And I'd agree—joy *is* frivolous.

But aren't your favorite memories the silliest ones?

Isn't your list of favorite people full of friends and family who make you smile and feel warm?

Think of the outfit that makes you feel most confident—you know, the one you reach for most often.

The creamer you're most likely to pull out of the fridge—why that one?

The coffee cup you will most likely pick tomorrow morning.

The song you put on repeat.

The best kinds of texts—the ones that make you giggle inside.

The step you chose to take to crunch leaves just because you like how it sounds.

The way your childhood self would look up at the sky and try to see shapes in the clouds.

Frivolous. Delightful. Wonderful.

But seeking out joy *is* the responsible next step to loving your life. You're making the most out of the moments. These build the résumé for joy that you'll one day refer to when you're wondering, like I was, how everyone else around you can be enjoying life when yours feels so tough.

Please hear me say this: these details are never meant to replace Jesus. We know that.

So why are they necessary? What makes the choices meaningful even as they feel meaningless? You may be wondering this like I once was.

Because when you choose to collect evidence of joy, you give other people the courage to do the same. Joy is contagious. It's not meant to fill the void and replace our need for Jesus; it's meant to magnify Him and make it known that He is in the details too.

Life is so much more complex than any of us would ever believe. This is the most beautiful part of the gospel to me—that God chose to come to earth to experience this complicated life, and when He did so, He found ways to delight in the details. He invited people to share meals, daily rhythms, encouragement, and conversations, even though He knew the pain that was to come.

So yeah, joy is rebellious. To find ways to harvest joy in the middle of your pain is to live in rebellion against what's always been true for our world while also holding the hope that there is more in store for us.

Responsibility is much more than taking life seriously. Sometimes it's taking life a little *less* seriously.

Confetti, Clinks, and Crying

After losing my dad, I fought for ways to keep his legacy alive. It took a while, and I wallowed in my grief for what felt like a decade—actually, it was a decade.

But once I woke up to the reality that he will only be kept alive by memories and celebrations, I knew I had to make a move. I have Thomas to thank for this one because it wasn't easy to do alone (a quick plug for finding "a person" to do the hard work with). Every year on my dad's birthday, we find a way to celebrate his life. Some years we drive around town while listening to a playlist of his favorite music. Other birthdays end with a pepperoni pizza and large Cokes—his favorite meal. My favorite birthdays, though, are the ones where we commit all the way to a party.

We did that last year.

On February 20, I took the boys to our local grocery store and let them pick out a balloon and cake to bring back home. Maddex, my three-year-old at the time, pointed at the carrot cake, and I felt the tears take a seat at the bottom of my eyes.

"Carrot cake—that's Granddaddy Bill's favorite," I exclaimed. "Good choice!"

We roamed the aisles for other groceries on our list, and every time a stranger asked, "Whose birthday is it?" the boys beamed and answered with their grandfather's name.

We got home, ate dinner as a family, and lit the candles on a birthday cake for a man the boys will never know—but whose legacy, I pray, they will never forget.

I wish I could say it was the typical fun celebration where wishes were made, the birthday person got a hug, and memories were shared. That wasn't our reality. It was still hard. I still found myself thinking, *I didn't sign up for this.* I cried hot, angry tears and had to answer hard toddler questions like "Why isn't Granddaddy Bill at his birthday party?"

That's the delicate part of unexpected tragedies and living with grief and trauma: it doesn't get easy. But it becomes more meaningful as the years go by.

A way to happen to life when it's happening to you: celebrate anyway. Make a fool of the grief and do the unexpected. Your heart needs it, your brain craves it, and your family and community will benefit from it. It's worth it.

Not only is joy possible in the midst of pain—it's essential. When we take the posture of joy and gratitude through pain, the world will think we've lost touch with reality—when actually we have the best grip on eternal reality we'll ever know this side of heaven.

CHAPTER 3

BREAKING AND ENTERING: WHEN JOY GETS JACKED AND HOW TO GET IT BACK

Splendor and majesty are before him;
strength and joy are in his place.

1 CHRONICLES 16:27

Every year during the last week of June, the whole Awtrey crew (grandparents, aunts, uncles, cousins, everybody) heads to the beach to spend a week together away, and it is always so refreshing! After the chaos of life, we had been holding out for this trip. Our friends even rooted us on by encouraging us to "just get to the beach" and then we would find rest.

We packed up our bags, threw them in the car, drove to the airport, and packed up the plane Thomas would be flying us in. He kept complaining that his stomach hurt but that he'd "be fine." Ladies, let's chat: I wasn't quite sure about the relative severity of his "pain," and I didn't know how seriously to take it all. Maybe some Pepto Bismol, some Gas-X would do?

Unfortunately, this was not the case. About thirty minutes before landing, we realized this was no ordinary stomach pain. Once we landed, we immediately passed our children over to the grandparents and headed to the closest emergency room. Sure enough, after a few warm blankets, beeping machines, blood work, and a CT scan, the doctor came back in and in one breath, casually told us: "Yep! Appendicitis. We'll admit you. IV of antibiotics overnight. Try to fit in a surgery tomorrow. We'll get that thing taken out. Keep you for a few hours to watch you. Hopefully we'll discharge you by the end of the day tomorrow. And then you can go home."

We blinked a few times. Made quick eye contact with one another. Blinked a few more times.

"Excuse me?"

We were stunned. The shock didn't last long once we grasped the reality of this stomach pain turning into appendicitis and emergent surgery on our vacation that we had been holding out for in order to rest.

We took a deep breath . . . and erupted into synchronous laughter. Maybe we were laughing so we wouldn't start crying. Once we were discharged and cleared to "go home" (the beach house for our vacation), the spiraling hit me.

Thomas may have had appendicitis, but I had discontentitis. Nothing felt good enough to get me out of the hole I was in. Have you ever been on a car hunt where you start looking up a certain vehicle—maybe even a certain year or color or with a certain feature—and before you know it, they pop up everywhere you look: online, in your neighborhood, on the road? It's not that they didn't exist before; it's that you didn't know to look for them. But now that your mind is thinking of this specific car, your eyes will start to see that car—everywhere. The same thing was happening with my vacation: for the next few days, everywhere I looked, there seemed to be something "wrong."

The sand bothered me more than it typically would.

Thomas couldn't pick up the boys with his postsurgical instructions, so I did a lot of heavy lifting. I was tired.

The house wasn't our own, so we were craving some familiarity we didn't have.

I surely saw everything I was looking for: all the hard stuff.

On a Scale of Typical to Tragic

Let's be honest: not all hard days are created equal. If we're on a journey to fight to find joy within our likable lives, it's important to first recognize there's a spectrum of reasons we may be struggling. Knowing the reason will ultimately determine our reaction. It's a bit like my orchid, Ophelia (who you might remember from the intro)—if I had known the reason for her demise was overwatering, I wouldn't have continued to add water to the pot. If you're just having a bad day filled with inconveniences—you're running late, the drive-thru line is long, and the kids are hangry . . . or your vacation isn't going according to plan—you wouldn't quit your job or move across the country. But if your world is shaken by tragedy, you might be more inclined to respond with drastic changes. Here's the scale of typical to tragic that we'll be exploring in this chapter:

Typical Interruptions	Everyday Stressors	Tough Seasons	Major Disruptions	Traumatic Events	Unexpected Tragedies

In the first part of the chapter, we're going to look at three different kinds of hard days and the ways they threaten our joy and contentment. (Check out the table on page 47 for how to identify other types of hard days you've probably experienced.) Then we'll explore how comparison sometimes adds to the equation and trips us up. But hold tight—the next few chapters are packed with all kinds of ways to fight back and infuse our lives with joy.

Typical Interruptions (or, the one where everything's annoying)

It was the perfect chili and corn bread kind of night. I texted a few of our closest friends and neighbors to ask if they wanted last-minute dinner plans, turned on my favorite cooking playlist, and started preparing what was about to be the best chili—after all, I had worked hard to perfect this recipe.

What really makes this chili *my chili* are the proportions: a little cumin, a little garlic powder, a pinch of cinnamon (you'll have to try it!), chili powder, onion powder, and the tiniest dash of cayenne—

NO NO NO NO! Not the whole jar of cayenne pepper! Who in the world doesn't put the sprinkle lid back on the spice jar?!

My Martha Stewart moment was rudely interrupted by an enormous pour of cayenne pepper—the heat and spice of this recipe—ruining it for anyone to eat except someone willing to breathe fire for the rest of the night.

I was ticked off. A huff of hot air filled my chest, and angry tears welled in my eyes.

It had already been a long day. And yes, I knew it wasn't *that* big of a deal—except that I also had a splotch of tomato sauce on my white top. And moments before, I had stepped on a Lego as I reached for the pot. And my toddler was providing an intense soundtrack with his new little drum set ten feet away from me. It all became a little . . . too much.

When we find ourselves in this category, our thoughts march to the tune of *Well, that's annoying.* The inconveniences of life pile up: your local grocery store stopped carrying your favorite granola on the same day that your baby fell asleep in the car and subsequently ruined your plan for a chill bedtime, and of course, you got a flat tire on the way to work. They're not day-ruiners, necessarily—until they are. You know what I mean.

Living with this mindset is tricky, because even though the inconveniences aren't big, they certainly *feel* that way in the moment. If they only matter to you, do they matter?

Spoiler alert—they do.

Tough Seasons (or, the one where the bad lasts longer than you'd like)

One of our temporary addresses during pilot training on my husband's Air Force journey was in a petite town in Oklahoma, and I'll say something that may be a bit unpopular: I think I'm officially not a Southwest girly. I wasn't used to the dust, the wind, the literal tumbleweeds, and the constant tornado warnings. Mix that with being thousands of *miles* away from our previous community, our family, and our friends—it was a really tough season.

The idea of "getting outside" felt so unrealistic.

I was not very happy, but I did my best to "soak it all in." After all, I was sitting in the baby stage with my new nine-month-old: the cute chubby legs and all. But over and over I was struck by how *permanent* this tough season felt. I was so buried by my current reality and the uncertainty of how long it would last (military life, am I right?) that I couldn't see through it.

This can't be forever, you may say or think at times like these. It's almost as if someone takes our snow globe of a life and shakes it up, and we have to wait for the "snow" to settle so we can see clearly once again. When your days are filled with wrangling a screaming seven-month-old baby into a car seat, you might think, *Surely he won't be eighteen years old and still crying in the car in between errands, right? RIGHT?!* Except it sure feels like he will. Or when you're in a dry spiritual season, you know God is real, but you don't feel Him closely. You open your Bible to do the "quiet time" you know

WHAT KIND OF HARD DAY IS THIS (AND HOW DOES IT THREATEN MY JOY)?

Category	*Examples*	*Characteristics*
Typical Interruptions	· Spilling coffee · Traffic jams · A forgotten deadline · A canceled lunch plan	· Short-lived · Low emotional impact · Frustrating but manageable
Everyday Stressors	· Miscommunication with a partner · Overwhelming workload · Running late frequently	· Recurring or ongoing · Causes noticeable frustration or fatigue · Resolvable with effort or time
Tough Seasons	· Postpartum adjustment · Relocation to a new city · Financial strain	· Requires adaptation · Often long-lasting · Feels burdensome but not insurmountable
Major Disruptions	· Loss of a job · Ending a long-term relationship · Serious illness in the family	· Significantly impacts daily life · Requires significant emotional and practical effort to manage
Traumatic Events	· Loss of a loved one · Experiencing abuse or violence · Living through a natural disaster	· Deeply distressing and overwhelming · May have long-term emotional, mental, or physical impacts
Unexpected Tragedies	· Chronic illness diagnosis · Surviving a catastrophic event · Major betrayal or loss	· Fundamental change to one's sense of self or future · Long-term healing or adjustment required

you're supposed to do before starting your day, but you don't even know where to start, what to read, which words to pray. And if you do read anything, you truly can't stop thinking about other tasks and future parts of your day. Or you sing the words of worship songs in church, but they're not making the journey from your head to your heart.

You don't know how your particular story is going to

end—and it's hard to see the forest for the trees while you wait.

Unexpected Tragedies (or, the one where life changes forever)

Chances are, if you read this heading, a story immediately comes to your mind. You feel it in your body—right in the gut—as the memory of the time life changed drastically comes rushing back.

The friend you lost suddenly—you didn't get the chance to say goodbye.

The multiple pregnancies you've lost and the hope you lost with them.

The loss of a career or dream that you were gripping tightly.

The diagnosis you received for your medically fragile child that changed life as you knew it.

The betrayal of someone in your community—or even of yourself.

The death of a marriage (yours or someone else's) that you were relying on for survival and function.

The despair of this mindset leaves you with one devastating thought on repeat: *This is my life now.* For me, a few memories come to mind: the accident that swooped my dad from the earth, the death of a dream after a betrayal, the baby I lost in pregnancy that I'll never know. There's a level of grief when something that once existed and was an essential part of our reality does not exist anymore—and it leaves a scar, a stain, that will require an explanation every now and then.

There's no escaping these moments. I've learned the hard way that it's not possible to steer clear, avoid, or manipulate life around devastating experiences like these. As much as the performer in me wants to imagine that tragic events from years ago didn't happen and that one might not happen tomorrow, there's not enough strength in my jaw to power through and pretend I can earn my free pass to wiggle around them. This can be hard to hear, but I hope you hear the grace in it too: there's nothing you can do to keep tragedies from happening. There's also nothing you can do to cause them—it's not your fault when these things happen. They're an inevitable part of life.

Don't Give Up

The first gift I remember opening myself as a child was on the shaggy carpeted floor of my Mimi and Grandy's home in Columbus, Georgia.

It was Christmas morning, and I was almost four years old. With my dad's hand in mine, I headed down the three steps at the end of the hall that stood between me and the presents I had been eyeing the night before.

Every loosening of the ribbon and tearing of the wrapping paper brought so much joy and excitement to see what was inside the first box. Maybe that's why I remember this gift more than any other before—or maybe it was because my Grandy had a camcorder pressed to the side of his face during these precious family moments and I've watched that home video many times.

But this particular present wasn't a gift from my wish list or a Barbie I had circled in a catalog. It was something I hadn't known I needed, but as soon as I laid eyes on it, it became my favorite: Rollerblades. Of course, there was a side gift of elbow and kneepads and a purple helmet that would come in handy for the afternoon that followed.

The four-year-old version of Rachel imagined my Rollerblading adventure unfolding much more smoothly than it did. I pictured the wheels rolling, me floating on top, and swiftly making it down the street like I had seen my older neighbors do in the past. However, my "roll" was more of a shuffle. Unless my dad took my hand, I only stood a four-second chance before I fell to my knees (or, even worse, on the muscle part of my palms). There were tears. There were lots of stops and pauses and trying again and "Take a deep breath" and "I quit!"s before we took our first break.

But after that trial run of what "Rollerblading Rachel" would be like, I knew more about myself. This experience started conversations with my dad about trying difficult things in life, getting up when I got knocked down, how to fall so I didn't hurt myself, the importance of a helmet, and many other life lessons.

I so wish this book were compiled of all the ways we could run from bad days, stay vigilant and three steps ahead so we never experience pain. I'm quick to buy the self-help books that emphasize all the practical tips and shortcuts to steer clear of sticky situations and confrontations and wiggle out of any moment that may make me flinch.

But to live a life constantly bubble wrapped, wearing a helmet with elbows and knees padded, is unrealistic, not abundant, and purposeless.

We would never be hurt in the ways that grow our compassion.

We would never know the warmth of a hug.

We would never get knocked to our knees and know the strength it takes to stand again.

We would never have to ask for help to heal.

We often go on our own "Rollerblading" adventures and end up hurt, bruised, and even scarred. We decide to put away the skates for good, and we never get better.

To this day, when I visit Grandy and Mimi, our go-to rainy-day activity is to pull out the old VHS tapes, DVDs, and home videos to rewatch and reminisce on the days that made our family what it is. I can almost tell you the time stamp of this Rollerblading moment because I'm so fond of the gift and the experience and the videos of my dad and me shuffling hand in hand down the street. He's patient, he's kind, he's giggling as I wipe my snotty tears to the side, he's winking at the camera to let my grandfather know we're okay.

I like to think this is the heart of our heavenly Father too. He knows when we're trying something that feels so hard—like going on the hunt for joy when life feels cluttered with despair. We're upset because we want it to be easier, frustrated with ourselves when we fall, but He's still grinning because He's so proud we even tried.

There's no pressure for us, His children, to live a life unscathed, perfectly performed, bowing at the end to roaring applause. It's the small, mundane moments that build up the space for God to breathe—even on days that aren't up to par.

If we yield to a counterfeit and compromised life that believes bad moments make a bad day and bad days have the final say, will we ever enjoy the gift of the rich life God has offered us? I hope we never have to know.

That four-year-old only put on the skates in the first place because she saw other people do it and have fun on their own Rollerblading adventures.

I pray we become so good at happening to life so it doesn't happen to us—that the passion and zeal we carry even in the midst of the hardest days is so evident and so contagious that others want to try it out too.

Morning Mistake

My feet hit the floor, and I thought to myself, *Oh my goodness! Oliver slept through the night!* He was nine months old, and it was still regular for him to wake up every three to four hours, needing a few cuddles to go back to sleep. I didn't realize it at first, but this routine was slowly turning me inside out, and I dreaded going to sleep, knowing I would be woken up as soon as I hit my first REM cycle.

This morning, everything felt a little different—in a good way. My coffee was a little silkier, the creamer tasted a little frothier, and the sun was shining a little brighter. Our kitchen felt like a lovely place to linger a few moments longer, soaking up the silence before the rest of the crew was up.

Ahhh, I thought. *A little moment to myself.*

So I did what I think a lot of us would do—I opened my phone, started checking the notifications that had come in overnight, and as muscle memory took hold of my finger, I blinked and my Instagram app was open.

An incredible house renovation was complete, and I was looking at the before and after pictures.

The beautiful couple I followed had traveled to Greece.

Her business looked like it was thriving.

The pediatric nutritionist I followed told me I wasn't giving my children enough protein in their breakfast.

My morning was lovely until . . . it wasn't.

My first mistake was thinking my life was so amazing at seven in the morning that nothing could get in my way. What I know to be true is that things will (and would) happen throughout the rest of the day that wouldn't be as glorious as the few moments of silence I got to myself while being able to "sleep in" and sip my coffee while it was hot. Deep down, I wasn't ignorant enough to think that the marvelous would outweigh the mundane and I'd be invincible the rest of the day.

My second mistake was almost too obvious, but I often miss it: I turned to the world to fill those first few moments instead of God's Word. Shame off me—and you—if this habit is one we struggle with. But I also can't help but wonder how my days would be different if I took a moment to pause, pray, reflect with gratitude, and meet with the Lord before anxiously filling my time with aimless scrolling or other purposeless pursuits.

I also have to wonder if the problem isn't that we don't have much to celebrate or our life isn't likable or that our hearts are discontent as much as we're distracted. Maybe distraction and comparison prevent us from seeing our lives clearly. Maybe her wardrobe, their vacation, that house's kitchen, and those children are deemed somehow "better" than ours, so our brain uses them as our unrealistic standard, and anything "less than" (or just different) is written off as mediocre.

Here's the truth: even if everything in our lives were "fixed" and beautiful on the outside—just like this particular morning was—we would struggle to find joy as long as we compared ourselves, our lives, our bodies, and our friendships.

Isn't it fascinating that when we live with the default of comparing ourselves (knowingly or unknowingly) to other people—whether online or in real life—we become exhausted and burned out, often giving in and giving up what we were once called to? I imagine it as running up the down escalator only to realize we haven't gone very far at all.

Comparison is the act of taking our eyes off who God is and fixing our eyes on ourselves instead. When we look inward instead of upward, we'll end up staring at scenes that were never meant for us to aim at as our "goal." We'll see joy that isn't ours, celebrations we missed out on, opportunities that went elsewhere, standards we don't meet. It makes a lot of sense why we don't love what we see when we hold our lives up to other people's highlight reels.

In the Bible, we read, "Think about the things of heaven, not the things of earth" (Colossians 3:2, NLT). God invites us to fix our thoughts on Him because He knows that's best for us. But the enemy likes to keep us distracted—to fix our eyes on anything other than what God intends for us to behold: Him and the victory we have in Jesus.

If we keep looking over *there*, watching them and wanting what they have, whether a relationship, a possession, or a position, it'll keep us so turned around, twisted, and confused that eventually we won't like where we've ended up and we'll be dissatisfied with where we're at. What a compromised way to live. In that case, the enemy wins.

When their marriage becomes your goal, you lose. When loving your own spouse and thanking the Lord for your marriage becomes your goal, you win.

When their house becomes your goal, you lose. When stewarding what *you* have well and celebrating their space with them becomes your goal, you win.

When their friendships become your goal, you lose. When seeking acceptance first in Jesus and overflowing from there becomes your goal, you win.

Maybe when we don't like our life, it has a lot to do with not liking what it looks like compared to what we see online and in the world around us.

Missed Expectations

Recently, I was cleaning up my nightstand and found the stack of journals I had kept for the first few years of our marriage. They were full of prayers, thanking the Lord for who God made Thomas to be, asking Him to move my heart and his in the same direction to an agreement on something we felt unsettled about—it was cute. There were short phrases that made me giggle and cringe all at the same time. In one moment, I thought, *That Rachel would never believe where this Rachel is now.* And in the next, in a more solemn tone, I thought, *Yeah, that Rachel would never believe where this Rachel is now.* Shame washed over me as I thought about the eager ideas I had dreamed up for our family that we're a few years behind on, the savings account that I thought would look different but doesn't because of a few emergencies. I thought about the current spiritually dry season I found myself in and the zeal for the Lord that the ink on that page held.

I really did think my husband and I would have our stuff together by now. You know—have our minds made up about all the adult decisions on our plate, or at least an idea of how to do them well.

In that moment, I felt an odd sense that I might be

missing out on a version of my life that I should be living, and before I knew it, I was comparing myself to an ideal version of myself.

Let me be clear about this: comparison doesn't always mean we're looking at others. I frequently think that comparing my circumstances to other people's is the furthest limit of what comparison is, when in reality it's the starting line. The sneakiest and most threatening type of comparison is when I try to evaluate the life I have in light of the life I thought I wanted.

I thought this season would look different than it does, and maybe you did too. Comparing the life I have with the life I thought I'd have keeps me from seeing the joy and contentment that's right in front of me.

I'm supposed to be married right now, you think, after attending *another* friend's wedding.

I'm supposed to have an idea of where my career is going, you think when you see someone get a job they love or mention something online about the next career move they're making.

I was supposed to have a child by now, you think at the holiday dinner table when your aunt asks you about your plan for starting a family.

I'm not supposed to be living paycheck to paycheck, you think, after paying another bill or making a hard decision not to spend money on something.

Comparison is the chasm between the expectation you had and what reality served you.

No "fix" can build the bridge to get us from one side of the canyon to the other. There's no amount of security in your friendships, coziness in your home, color in your wardrobe, consistency in your routine that could bring you the joy you're missing if this crucial issue is not dealt with.

Just because this season turned out *unlike* you thought it would doesn't mean your whole life is *unlikable*.

Can I ask you a few questions that I really want you to wrestle with?

Who are you getting your standards and timelines from?

What could you be missing that's right in front of you when you choose to look to the left and to the right?

What do you believe about God to be true?

When we honor God with our yes and our no, no matter what life looks like compared to what we thought it would, we can trust that He knows what is best for us.

There are moments, God-winks, and details in all our lives that God wants us to delight in—little gifts, if you will, that act as the breadcrumbs to a life that's able to be liked if we look where our feet are instead of focusing on where they're not.

Like the moment you start to feel lonely and a friend sends you a voice message full of affirmation. Or when the person in front of you in the drive-thru pays for your coffee. Or when you stumble across your favorite flowers, which you've never noticed on your daily walk. Can I remind you that God has everything we need—infinite resources and a comprehension of our life that we'll never fully understand?

The mystery can be frustrating at times, but it's worth leaning into. God has a life reserved for *you.* Nothing you say or do can make it happen any more quickly or slowly. Nothing you say or do can change who God is. His timing is impeccable. He is the same yesterday, today, and forever (see Hebrews 13:8). It's always better to surrender our lives and yield our desires, plans, and expectations to God and see what He will do with them. As Ephesians 3:20 says, God "is able to do far more abundantly than all that we ask or think."

He can do more than we could ever imagine.

He will use it for His glory.

He will work it out for our good.

Different Gifts

When we moved to Birmingham, one of my first friends was an incredible pal who was like a big sister to me. She's kind, considerate, the greatest host, seriously talented in the kitchen, and I just think she's the coolest. From the items she has in her pantry and fridge to the home decor and accessories she found at a thrift store to the way her house smells to the way she decorates, it's all lovely. She's warm, inviting, so authentic and likable. She's the mom who has the playdate with the Pinterest snacks and hors d'oeuvres labeled with signs.

I think many times, when I try to describe what comparison is or the person I'm comparing myself to, I think of Meredith Blake to my Annie (*The Parent Trap*) or Regina

George to my Cady Heron (*Mean Girls*)—in other words, my intimidating adversary. In reality, though, comparison is usually much slyer. We may be tempted to compare ourselves to the friends who are closest to us—who mean the most to us and bring us the greatest comfort.

Should I be parenting like that?

That's not what I made for dinner.

I don't work out as much as she does.

My job doesn't have those benefits.

Sometimes the people we're closest to can be the easiest objects of our comparison. It may seem harmless, but comparison creates fractures in friendship, isolation instead of intimacy, and discontent instead of delight.

Discontent through comparison obscures our joy by keeping us focused on what God is doing for someone else rather than what He's doing in our own lives. In the book of Romans, Paul writes, "We all have different gifts that God has given to us by His loving-favor. We are to use them. If someone has the gift of preaching the Good News, he should preach. He should use the faith God has given him" (12:6, NLV). But it's only too easy to overlook our own gifts—and how we can serve God with them—when we compare our life to someone else's.

Let me make this very clear: someone else's likable life cannot threaten the likability of yours unless you let it. Here are a few truths I remind myself of when I start turning inward after being around someone else's likable life and begin to think that mine, because it's different, is less than.

Everything comes at a cost.

It's easy for us to forget that what someone has (or doesn't have) comes with a lot of closed-door conversations, sacrifices, and situations that we may not want to sign up for. A process happens before the product, and as much as I may want the product, I'm slow to sign up for the process it would take to get there.

There's no formula.

There's no recipe, reward system, or map that would ever help us fully understand the differences between our life and someone else's. God is omniscient and omnipotent, meaning He is both all-knowing and all-powerful. He is the One who controls what happens and when it happens. Ultimately, it isn't possible for us to manipulate our lives into the shape we want them to take, so the best posture for us is a surrendered one.

God has more than enough.

He is not withholding anything good from you. As Psalm 84:11 says, "For the LORD God is a sun and shield; the LORD will give grace and glory; no good thing will He withhold from those who walk uprightly" (NKJV). In the moments we feel like there is nothing to enjoy in our lives, it's not because God is keeping something from us but because we aren't seeing His gifts. Let's ask God to help us find joy in what He's given us and not try to figure out why He hasn't given us the same gifts He gave someone else.

Cut to the Chase

There are so many ways to understand why we compare ourselves to others, but sometimes I need practical over hypothetical. *Give me some rules! Boss me around!* I often think.

So, my friend, here are a few practical steps that I work through when I find myself in the corner of comparison:

1. I pay attention to what I'm watching, listening to, and looking at. I practice an audit of my online entertainment when I find myself comparison prone. I unfollow accounts that tempt me to compare instead of helping me see beauty where I am. Or I comment and cheer others on to fight the impulse of comparison.
2. I try to notice the small things and go on a treasure hunt for what I have that I'm grateful for. This helps me prove to myself that I'm thankful for my life when I start slipping back into the trap of comparison. How about *Both of our lives can be wonderful in different ways*?
3. When I really can't notice much about my own life that I like, I ask my friends for their input. "What do you love about my life? I need help calling out the likable parts I haven't noticed." You'll hear beautiful things in response.
4. I try to experiment with a spending freeze and ask myself, *Am I trying to fill the void of comparison by*

adding things to cart, or am I truly going to the Lord and asking Him to help me be content? Usually, not spending money on items I don't really need directs me to an answer.

5. When I have a hard time being in the "right place" with someone because she has something I desire, I congratulate her and actually mean it. Putting praise on your lips is one of the best expressions of *God, I can see your goodness in their life* even when you're struggling with contentment in your own life.

Mornings like the one I described earlier in this chapter still happen. I wake up surprised by how well I slept, I remember an exciting event that's happening that day—like an adventure I had planned for my family or a thrilling work meeting—or I open a text from a friend about something incredible happening in her life. But I also experience moments that interrupt the joy with thoughts of could-haves and should-haves that come quickly to steal my moment of rejoicing. And now, instead of defaulting to defeat and hanging my head low, heavy with jealousy and resentment, I lift it again and pray:

What's theirs is meant for them. What's mine cannot be taken from me. I thank you, Jesus, for showing Yourself through their life in that way and I ask that You'd reveal Yourself to me today as well. I surrender this moment, these feelings, and my life to You and return to the truth in knowing that You are a good Father who gives good gifts, even if I'm not the one to receive them. Amen.

A Break in the Clouds

Once people find out that Thomas is a pilot and that we fly as a family in a small aircraft, I can almost guarantee they'll say, "Do you get nervous flying with him?" or "Tell me about one of the scariest times you flew together." We've been on a few aviation adventures—and I have enough trust in my back pocket to whip out any time I start to get nervous—but one flight in particular comes to mind when I'm asked to tell a story.

First, you should know that there are two types of flying: VFR and IFR. VFR (visual flight rules) is the fun way to fly: by sight, so you can make decisions based on what you see out the windows in clear weather. IFR (instrument flight rules) is the not-so-fun way to fly when you have poor visibility conditions like fog, rain, or darkness, and you have to trust your instruments to tell you which way is up. IFR is the kind of flying where you can find me tightening my seat belt, putting my book away, and gripping Thomas's shoulder when we start to hit a few bumps.

On this flight, I was prepared for some rainy conditions. The skies over Birmingham were gray, and the clouds were dense, weighed down by oncoming rainstorms.

"We've gotta get up quick and break through the weather," Thomas said.

And with his calm, steady nature, he radioed the ground frequency and told them we'd be rolling onto the runway and taking off shortly.

I tried to swallow the lump in my throat—this was the first time we had flown through weather that we could see from the ground.

The engine roared.

The wheels started to squeak.

"Takeoff power is set. Airspeed is alive. Engine instruments are in the green," Thomas recited.

And we were off. Some pockets of air were thicker than others, so we rode the clouds like a boat on choppy water.

I watched the droplets form on my window and get pulled away by the wind whipping past.

I saw the clouds—which looked so solid—dissolve as our propeller sliced right through them.

The sky was dark and overcast, and the air looked thick.

Until it didn't.

All of a sudden, there was a clear break in a cloud that we aimed right through. On top of the cloud we climbed was a sliver of blue sky. We chased it. We set our sights on getting to the blue sky, above the clouds, where the sun would warm our windows again and dry up the droplets hanging on still.

And when we arrived in the open sky after minutes of climbing through the passage from takeoff to this moment, there was instant peace.

It can be difficult and go against every grain to believe that there are blue skies above a layer of clouds when you're standing with your feet on the ground. But once you gain elevation and perspective, you can see things more clearly.

We cannot believe the faulty idea that all we can see is all there is. There's so much more.

We can't let our bad days and moments of comparison have the final say. The break in the clouds is on its way.

PART TWO

joy on repeat

building a life you love

CHAPTER 4

AND 5, 6, 7, 8: OUR NEED FOR RHYTHMS

Are you tired? Worn out? Burned out on religion? Come to me. Get away with me and you'll recover your life. I'll show you how to take a real rest. Walk with me and work with me—watch how I do it. Learn the unforced rhythms of grace. I won't lay anything heavy or ill-fitting on you. Keep company with me and you'll learn to live freely and lightly.

MATTHEW 28:11, MSG

Have you ever noticed that we were created with natural rhythms? Heartbeats, the pace of our footsteps when we walk, the way we read a poem, the way we go to sleep at night and wake up in the morning. We were made to follow these rhythms.

Implementing rhythms in our lives helps bring order to chaos. It gives us margin to take a deep breath (or sometimes to catch our breath) when life feels too fast. It gives us a chair to rest on in the middle of the race and mile markers so we know how far we've gone and when to speed up or slow down. Rhythms give us predictability and standards to use for what we consider normal. This way, when opportunities come, pivots happen, or unpredictability greets us at the worst times, we know what belongs where and what doesn't belong at all.

When we hold time and rhythms loosely yet strategically, something beautiful happens: we create space for spontaneity, discernment, and obedience to come more easily. Isn't that the life we all want to live?

In many parts of life, we crave the structure, the predictability, the comfort of knowing what to expect. Imagine if the grocery store were rearranged every time we went to grab produce or if the interstate exit signs were labeled differently every day for your commute or even (heaven forbid) if your already-unorganized pantry were further disorganized in such a way that you couldn't find the ingredients for supper. My eye is starting to twitch just thinking about this.

Although the grocery store isn't usually switched up and the exit signs aren't wildly different from day to day, life does ask us to bend more than we'd like. So how do we bend in such a way that we don't break? We seek consistency where we can to ground ourselves when the unseeable and uncontrollable shows up, as we know it will. But maybe the unpredictable, unsolvable, and inconsistent isn't our foe. Even the best songs have a key change and a bridge that divides the verse from the chorus.

That's life too.

You can still like your life and find joy right where you are, even when the song changes key or the bridge starts unexpectedly. These interruptions don't always mean the end of something good. All rhythms change eventually. But rhythms must exist in the first place if we are to embrace change and see it as an opportunity rather than an intrusion.

Everyday Rhythms and Habits

I'd like to think that once we had a rhythm figured out, it would stick around for good. The thing about rhythms, though, is that sometimes we need to change our mind, pivot, or switch it up. Unlike our natural physical rhythms, the patterns we choose are up to us—we must discern what works best. When we don't like something about our lives, it may be time to take a step back and evaluate how our rhythms are rocking and rolling. When life feels clunky, it's tough to enjoy it, but when life is mostly in order, we have a bit more capacity to handle the chaos when it comes.

You know those moments when you've pushed off something with a firm due date until the last minute, and then it creeps up on you, asking you to hurry, rush what's important, compromise in areas you wish you could be excellent in?

Been there.

Or maybe organization is not your strong suit, so those projects weren't delayed on purpose but rather . . . forgotten about completely?

Also been there.

How about the seasons when "life is life-ing" and you're asked to stretch in ways that you really don't have the flexibility for but wish you did?

I get it.

Here are just a few ideas for how to establish healthy, functional rhythms to make your daily life more joyful.

Notice what isn't working—and what is.

What used to work for you may not work any longer. And that's okay. You're allowed to change your mind, choose a different plan of action, and try something new. If we don't take a minute to hit pause and evaluate where we are in life—what's working well and what's not—it can be hard to pinpoint what's wrong. When we take inventory, we will likely have some "aha" moments and figure out how to move obstacles out of our way that we've been used to charging through or jumping over. Your future self will thank you.

When moving back "home" from Oklahoma after our pilot training journey, we had the opportunity to start fresh and take inventory of many things in our lives that we'd be returning to.

This sparked questions like *Do we want to do that the same way as before?*

Will we continue to go to church there?

Are those friends still the friends we can count on returning to?

Even down to *Is this the house we want to move back into?*

Having that clean slate was a luxury even though we were overwhelmed by it, but it prompted us to change our minds about what had been begging to be different from the beginning—we just needed the "permission" to switch it up.

And as we started diving into the larger-scale questions, our everyday habits became a part of the conversation too.

The moment I knew I needed to stop, pause, and reflect, I gained insight into my life that truly stopped me in my tracks. I found answers to why it was difficult to manage my time (because I wasn't using my calendar), why it was hard for me to get dinner on the table when everyone was hungry (because I hadn't planned what we would eat), and why my closet continued to get more disorganized (because I didn't have a place for things, so they just got stuffed where there was a void big enough for them).

When I figured out what was working, I was able to keep it in place and really embrace it and get a boost from it. When I labeled what was malfunctioning, I could give it the attention needed to alter it accordingly.

I realize that not everyone has a "closing of a chapter" situation in their own life (like moving or some other milestone) that initiates needed change. But I wonder if we're waiting for those moments to happen before we change what we already feel called to change, whether monumental or mundane.

Make your decisions easier.

"Where do you want to go to dinner?" is probably the worst way to start a date night, in my opinion. By that point, I've made decisions all day. From the moment I woke up, I've been choosing what I'd feed my family, what route to take home to avoid traffic, what I should wear that would be comfortable for the day ahead. I've had to make logistical calls about birthdays, meetings, and other "life things." So by the end of the day, I'm fatigued. Not necessarily physically, although sometimes. Let's call it decision fatigue.

I wanted to believe this could be easier. After I took the step of noticing what was tricky for me, I realized decisions like where to eat weren't just one-time struggles. They tended to come up regularly. Every day I have to choose something to make for dinner. Every day I have to find an outfit in my cluttered closet. So what if I could make one decision that would make the other decisions easier? As my author friend Kendra Adachi (the Lazy Genius) says, "Decide once"![1]

Maybe Fridays are always pizza dinners and Sundays are leftovers only.

Maybe you have an overwhelming number of sweatshirts all over the place, so you decide to stick them all in one drawer.

Maybe there's a sports practice on an afternoon that feels chaotic every week, so you pack and prep the car the night before.

If you have a recurring decision to make in your life, decide once about it. When we have a way to operate in the small decisions, the bigger decisions get easier. We have the appropriate margin to handle them with the care they need rather than being so fatigued that we aren't able to be clearheaded and in tune with what God is asking of us in those moments. When we have the type of energy where we can make the big decisions prayerfully and be spontaneous because there's order where needed and we're not looking down the whole time trying to solve problems, we can look up and notice more around us. Naturally, this gives us a perspective that makes joy easier to find and life easier to love.

Here are some of the Awtrey family's "decide once" rules:

- Every time we travel through an airport and it's time to eat lunch, we look for a Chinese spot. Deciding this in advance and sticking to it eliminates bickering and bad attitudes about food.
- I rotate between two dresses for baby showers to avoid the "I have nothing to wear!" crisis right before I'm supposed to leave.
- A "church bag" hangs on our garage doorknob, waiting for me to grab it when we head to a Sunday service or Bible study. It has everything we typically need and gives me a little more brain space on an otherwise rushed morning.

These are just a few suggestions that work well for my family. Take a look at the chaotic corners of your own life and think, *How can I decide once to make this feel a little less stressful and a little more joyful?*

You don't have to do it how she does it.

One of our first arguments as a married couple revolved around how someone (no names here) loaded the dishwasher. Silly and petty—as most newlywed tiffs are. But it was interesting that differences in how we do things could evoke such emotion about our way being "right" or "wrong."

We all have our own perception of the world and how it works for us. It becomes easy to project that reality onto everyone else when really, the rhythms and routines that work for one person may not work for all.

How I organize my spice drawer may be significantly different from how yours is arranged. And you'd probably be appalled at my Tupperware drawer because I just throw everything in there. It fits that way, and it doesn't stress me out. What if the same principle were applied to how we operate in our rhythms of life? I bet we would change many things. If you're anything like me, you've probably assumed one or more of the following to be "the way things are done":

"Dinner should be eaten at the dining room table."
"Exercise happens at the gym."
"Kids' toys belong in the playroom."
"Work should be done at a desk."
"Books go on a bookshelf."
"Shoes belong in the closet."

And so on and so forth. But are these statements true? Or are they based on expectations from who knows where and assumptions that often guide us to make decisions that actually don't work very well?

Our family does not keep our shoes in the closet. We used to until we realized we were always going up and down the stairs to grab shoes, socks, and other last-minute things.

We keep "bathroom items" such as sunscreen, hair care for the children, and deodorant in our entry table for easy access when we're on the way out the door.

The boys' toys are scattered all over the house, but you'd never know because we've found baskets with lids that double as decor and make everyone happy.

We sometimes switch up meals and eat them outside on a picnic blanket or even on the living room floor because, heck, we need a change every once in a while.

Maybe doing things the way they've always been done—the way she does it and the way it "should" be done—is what's causing the clunkiness.

The dog still needs to go outside, last-minute guests still come over, plans are still rescheduled, and I, too, still spill my coffee on my top as I walk out the door. These things will always happen, and the unpredictability can really rock us if we don't have good rhythms in place and the saved-up capacity for life to "life" once in a while. But noticing what's working and what's not, deciding once where we can, and seeing the freedom in doing things in the way that serves us best is what grants us a little wiggle room and makes life more functional and joyful on a day-to-day basis.

Rhythmic Routines

I'm not always about rules, as they can be too rigid, and like I've mentioned—some things don't work for everybody. But I am about research, and the research on rhythms in life shows that a bit of routine will contribute to a life you love.

Rhythms, routine, and order are not new ideas. They're ancient ideas that go all the way back to the beginning of time. In Genesis, God created our world with order in mind. Everything about Creation was orderly, from the sequence God chose, to the words He used, to His decision to rest once it was all accomplished. If God prioritizes order in the way He runs the world, surely it makes sense for us to seek order in our lives too. I'd like to share what orderly rhythms look like in my life, broken down into four different time frames. Hopefully these spark ideas for routines that will work for you!

In Our Days

In the Awtrey family, our morning and evening routines are held pretty loosely, but they're predictable enough that even when a day is tough, I can count on these bookends being in place. Mornings: I brew coffee, drink water, take vitamins, and ice-roll my face. Then the kids get up, I make their breakfast, read my Bible, and the day falls into place from there. Evenings: I tuck the boys into bed, go downstairs, do a few chores, drink more water, spend time with Thomas, do my skin-care routine, leave my phone downstairs (ideally), pray, and go to bed.

In Our Weeks

Each week, it's key for us to find a day to play and a day to rest. We've established rhythms that incorporate sports, church events, work, friend commitments, etc. Once you determine which weekly commitments are "set," you can add routines that give you some structure in the middle areas too. For us, our weeks look pretty "usual," and this allows room for us to change and add if needed.

We have childcare on predictable mornings, we have standing date nights every Tuesday evening, I host a small group of college students on Wednesday nights, Thursday evenings are our home group for church, and the other nights are family nights. During the days, we have scheduled practices for sports, I have standing meetings, and Thomas flies off and on for work. It's a both/and of order and rescheduling, communication and last-minute happenings. We know what's typical and expected, and because of this, we're able to check the pulse of our family and make the decisions necessary for each day. We build the schedule and prayerfully go throughout each day to see how it needs to change and shift.

In Our Months

I like to set aside a day each month to take inventory and get a pulse on how things are going in my life spiritually, emotionally, physically, financially, and relationally. This gives me a good idea of where things need to shift, pivot, or be thrown out completely if they're not serving this particular season of my life well. Once a month, I also love to get away to do something for myself. Maybe it's a trip, or maybe it's an afternoon alone grocery shopping or choosing not to add *anything* to the calendar. A well-rounded monthly routine benefits from days like these.

In Our Years

A yearly reflection has been so kind to our family. We're able to be still enough to give God the credit for coming through in hard situations. We evaluate the good habits we've created that need to stay and the bad ones that need to go. Thomas and I take a "selah" (pause) each year, and it's an event we always look forward to. Typically, we'll scoot away to a tree house just outside Chattanooga to rest and talk, phones aside, uninterrupted. It has been well worth the time away to get clarity on what is next for us. The movement in our hearts that happens in these sacred moments has carried our family through years we never saw coming. Other times, checking in with one another looks like taking a walk while we have a neighbor or trusted friend sit with the boys while they sleep. Some moments of rest without going anywhere seem so simple, they're easily overlooked: sitting outside, going for walks like I mentioned above, or finding a park in your town to take a meal to and have conversation over a switch of scenery.

A Disrupted Rhythm

There have been moments in my life—recently even—when I crave a routine but can't get it going in the way I want. From my husband's demanding job to raising babies (when the clock just doesn't mean anything anymore) to dealing with crises that scream for my immediate attention, life isn't always predictable. Disrupted rhythms are natural, unavoidable, and necessary for our individual growth.

If your ability to implement rhythms and routines has been disrupted, I'd love to suggest making a list of the top four things that would make for a successful day, no matter what else happened (or didn't happen). I call this version of me "low power mode." Like a device, when I'm running on little battery power and life demands more than I can give, I focus on what's necessary and give it all I've got. The other areas that are lower priority become fuzzy, slow, and glitchy—and I'm okay with that, because on low power mode it is to be expected. If you find yourself in this level of operation with me, be kind to yourself, and don't be overeager. Setting big goals to springboard you out of anything you're sitting in may not be the answer. Try small steps, identify the things that need to be prioritized, and *get specific*.

- Read my children a book
- Make my bed
- Listen to the Bible on audiobook
- Drink x amount of water

Being specific about the goals we have in mind when we're craving structure gives us the nudge that we *can* show up, even when life is different and difficult and disrupted. It also gives us something to celebrate when it's accomplished—even the mundane.

Isaiah 30:21 tells us, "Whether you turn to the right or to the left, your ears will hear a voice behind you, saying, 'This is the way; walk in it'" (NIV). How beautiful and fitting that we have the Holy Spirit to live inside of us, to act as our guide when life feels so cluttered we don't know what's deserving of our attention and time. If we lean in, pray for discernment, and follow the nudges, I wonder if we would find the routines and rhythms falling into place where we least expected them.

And last, when your rhythm feels disrupted, I urge you to hold on to the people around you, to borrow their rhythms and songs and let them remind you of truth regardless of what life is yelling around you. Other people can be the drums and percussion and metronome to our song. When we lose count, when we lose our place or forget the lyrics, they help keep the song going.

Having a routine and rhythms doesn't mean you're so strict you can never pivot. A structure makes it easier to be flexible because you can effectively prioritize elements of your day and see where they belong and where they don't, when they're possible and when they're not. You can give your best yes and best no when you have a rhythm in your life that is predictable for your body and mind.

The importance of rhythms in our lives is not only reserved for the type A, control-freak achievers who need to feel like they can micromanage their lives. What we do is who we are. The choices we make are building up our character and how we're known to others. Doing something once is a choice, doing something several times is a habit, but doing something repeatedly will become your character. Rhythms go beyond just having an easy, enjoyable life. They speak to the gift of order we have access to every day.

In the book of Proverbs, we read, "We can make our plans, but the LORD determines our steps" (16:9, NLT). We can't mess up what God has planned for us. (Imagine taking a pencil eraser to a permanent marker.) However, life is already so unpredictable, it's important to have some sort of synchrony to our lives and to steward the time we have well through rhythms and routines.

A Bad Case of the Hiccups

Life is hard—I get it. Some days are harder than others. Some hard days turn into weeks, and those turn into months and years and seasons. But some of the funkiest reasons we don't love our life are because we let small yet annoying inconveniences disrupt our routines and get in our way. These typical interruptions can add up quickly.

You get rear-ended on the exit ramp two minutes from your house.

You get a text that was not meant for you to read.

The dog barks at the mailman and wakes up the baby you just got down for a nap.

You see a picture with a group of friends at a party you were not invited to.

The person from the date you thought went well last night has not responded to your message.

Your computer freezes in the middle of an important meeting.

You lose your keys.

You didn't get the promotion you thought was yours.

One little thing adds to another, which adds to another, and before you know it you are done. Countless times, I've found myself leaning over the counter with my head in my hands, wondering how in the world it's already been such a hard day and it's only 10:13 a.m. You might hear these petite disruptions referred to as hiccups. I like that comparison a lot. Your body takes over, your diaphragm finds a rhythm that is so unhelpful, offbeat, and frustrating, and you just want to catch your breath.

It's in those hard moments that I can turn from calm to catastrophic more quickly than I'd like to admit.

Will I ever stop hiccupping?! Will I ever breathe like a normal human again?

I turn small problems into big problems, sometimes knowingly and sometimes unknowingly. I give them more credit than they're due. This is what some people call "getting worked up" or "spiraling" or (the psychological term) "ruminating." And before I know it, I'm stuck in a funk that no amount of "fun" could convince me out of.

Enough days like this, and it's easy to think you don't like the way your life is shaking out.

But here's the thing: hiccups don't last forever. Eventually our mind gets distracted enough or there's an interruption that allows our body to take a deep breath, find the rhythm that makes breathing comfortable again, and move on. Same goes for a typical inconvenience. But is it possible to interrupt the interruptions and not let them become part of our patterns?

Get Out of Your Funk

"I think I'm just in a funk," I told my friend Carla over a latte at a new coffee shop we were trying.

"It would make a lot of sense why."

It was the first time I had gotten out of the house for a while. I was a little in over my head with a few work projects and was carrying a lot of home responsibility while Thomas was away at a training he needed for his job. It did make sense to feel the way I did, but I couldn't see that clearly because I had no extra capacity. So I believed this: *I have no more margin for myself. Head down. Hustle forward. Do the work and get through it.*

What I wasn't seeing—until Carla brought the clarity—was

that life had just been funky, and it was going to take me to interrupt the funky rhythms.

So I headed home, planning the interruption I knew I needed to create. On my way, I stopped at the grocery store and picked up my kids' favorite popsicles. When I pulled into the driveway, I opened the garage and wheeled out the double stroller. It was time for a walk. My barefoot, half-dressed babies were tossed into the stroller and buckled up. I handed over the popsicles, and we were off. I turned on some worship music on my phone and placed it in the back of the stroller. Then I just opened my eyes a little wider to what was around me and listened to the giggles coming from the front, trying to not be absorbed by the fact that I would have to clean up melted popsicle juice on the stroller later that evening. It was worth it in that moment. It was turning our day around, one degree at a time.

It's important that I make sure we're on the same page and help you decipher what a funk is and how it's different from long-term mental health struggles. A funk feels like a temporary mood dip, whereas a struggle with mental health, such as anxiety or depression, is much more persistent and severe. I've been in both camps and want to hug you if the difference between these two is even something you're deciphering. Please take the help you need and find guidance on page 183.

In case you need some ideas of how to get out of a funk you find yourself in right now (or for the next time one strikes), feel free to borrow my list:

Nourish your body.

How many days have I been frazzled and on the fritz—and then I hear my stomach rumble and realize I'm running on two lukewarm cups of coffee and three bites of my kids' frozen waffles? It's embarrassing, to say the least.

We talk a lot about taking care of our hearts and our minds. But if we aren't taking care of the body they both live in, it can be easy to feel like a shell of a human rounding the bend toward a funk. This is part of the equation that can make a fine day a bad day or a bad day a worst day.

Listen, it's going to happen. The goal here is not to have a breakfast of eggs, sausage, and toast every morning and drink our weight in ounces of water and apply all the magazine-worthy health hacks. The goal is consistency, kindness, and awareness of what our body needs. If you're anything like me, when I become aware of how I've been neglecting my own nourishment, I can be tempted toward shame. (*You're a grown woman and know better, Rachel. You're failing at life.*) But I wonder what it would look like to choose compassion, to talk to ourselves like we would a friend? (*You had a lot going on today, Rachel. It makes sense why you forgot. You can try again tomorrow.*) Just try again.

Turn on music and dance.

My brother-in-law recently reminded me of all the beautiful moments that surfaced on social media during the pandemic in 2020. We saw viral videos from large metro areas like San

Francisco, New York City, and Chicago, where people flung open their balcony doors and grabbed the instruments they found in their homes—from guitars to keyboards to pots and pans. They sang popular songs to one another to lighten reality, find a moment of comfort and respite, and care for each other from afar. In these videos, you could see some people closing their eyes as they reclined and took in the symphony of strangers. Some treated their patios like dance floors, while others hummed and offered harmony.

It didn't change the conditions of the world. It didn't heal those who were suffering from COVID. But it did offer a moment of reprieve, a pause, a thinner layer between one neighbor and the other.

Music is an ancient art, and the Bible describes it being used for reassurance, perspective shifts, a change of season and circumstance, celebration, and more. It reminds us that we can actually experience joy where we are. How beautiful that God designed a way to move our body, our spirit, and our heart with the act of worship through song! Here are just a few of the many ways Scripture describes the value of music:

> What am I to do? I will pray with my spirit, but I will pray with my mind also; I will sing praise with my spirit, but I will sing with my mind also.
>
> 1 CORINTHIANS 14:15

Be filled with the Spirit, addressing one another in psalms and hymns and spiritual songs, singing and making melody to the Lord with your heart.

EPHESIANS 5:18-19

Let the word of Christ dwell in you richly, teaching
and admonishing one another in all wisdom,
singing psalms and hymns and spiritual songs,
with thankfulness in your hearts to God.

COLOSSIANS 3:16

Sometimes music is all we need to get out of a funk. And this can look lots of different ways:

- Roll your windows down and listen to a song from your childhood.
- Create a playlist to help yourself work through your feelings.
- Dance in the kitchen, alone or with the company of those you share it with.

It might seem a bit odd to get out of a funk this way, but sometimes we have to shake things up with intentional interruptions. It's hard to get bogged down or take ourselves too seriously when we choose to dance in the middle of distress.

Ground yourself.

How kind that God—the God who created the universe and every one of us—made us to find healing, joy, and rhythm in the natural world. He's an expert in what He created, so it makes perfect sense that one part of His creation can positively impact another part. God wants us to get out of our funks and into healthy routines. He wants us to live in abundance and freedom, and His gift of nature—sand, dirt, grass, snow, water, trees, wind, sunshine, birds, and animals—helps us do just that.

- Feel the sun's rays on your arms.
- Stand in the rain and feel the drops that land on you.
- Put your feet in the grass and notice if it's all plush and soft or if there are a few rough edges underneath.
- Listen to the sounds all around you: neighbors laughing, dogs barking, birds chirping, wind whistling, rain hitting the roof.
- As each new season arrives, pay attention to the distinct sounds underfoot. Hear the rustle of the leaves. Feel the crunch of the snow under your boots. Splash through the puddles.
- Notice.

Experiencing nature with your senses tells your body you're safe and the problems that surround you don't determine your reality. When those pesky hiccups in life happen, it's easy to get so pulled out of reality that we have a hard time understanding what is actually real and what our mind has made up, what is actually safe and what our mind has convinced us is dangerous, what is actually helpful and what is not helping us at all.

Start by simply putting your feet on the earth. Barefoot is great, but getting outside in any capacity is what we're going for.

My heart feels like it beats more effortlessly.

My mind feels clearer after stepping outside of the four walls of my home.

The air wakes my skin and the sun refreshes my eyes.

I just feel . . . aligned. And the happenings of the day fall into place.

Emotions Need Motion

I once heard it said, "Emotions need motion."

It's fascinating how that works too. When we get moving, our brain has the space to enter a new level of understanding and clarity. The back-and-forth movement of your body allows you to see things for what they are and understand them clearly.

Working my heart rate up *on purpose* and then allowing my body to find its natural beat again melts away my tension. Stretching my muscles gives me more agility throughout my day. Lifting weights and challenging myself to one more rep than I thought I could handle or planking for a few seconds longer than last time proves to my brain that I can overcome hard things. It's interesting that what we partake in physically often reflects what's happening in our minds and hearts.

"Sweat it out" and "Let's go for a walk" are some of the most helpful recommendations someone can give me when I present them with a low I'm working through. Cardio challenges, tennis with a friend, running your favorite trail, walking in your neighborhood with your dog or by yourself, jumping rope, taking a dance class, cycling, trying a new fitness studio, lifting weights—the options are endless.

A lot of us have reserved the idea of "movement" as a way to hit a goal, to make room for a treat later, or to punish ourselves for what we ate yesterday. But what if we looked at movement as a new way of finding freedom from a funk and getting back on track with our routines? We can prove to ourselves we're stronger than we thought we were, celebrate the idea that we can move our bodies, and find the fun in physical activity again.

Listen, a funky problem is relative. If you were to attempt these strategies when sitting in a tough season or trying to make it through the day after a tragedy, dancing in a kitchen and drinking some water might not change much about how you feel.

Creating a life we love requires us to move in rhythms, but not just for the sake of comfort, consistency, or convenience. Rather, rhythms allow us to see out-of-the-blue events as organic opportunities to glimpse God's fingerprints rather than dizzying and derailing disruptions. The moments that act as guardrails to our life grant us margin for the energy we need for choosing differently and using discernment for how things can be switched up, started, or stopped.

Musical rhythms can still hold crescendos and key changes that give goose bumps to listeners. The rhythms of the ocean can be dangerously powerful. And the rhythms that our body subconsciously chooses every breathing moment of our day sustain life. The rhythms of our days are a crucial part of living a life full of wonder, spontaneity, and zeal.

CHAPTER 5

HOW GOING SLOW MADE ME STEADY

Return to your rest, O my soul.
For the Lord has been good to you.

PSALM 116:7, NLV

Have you ever moved too fast in life to try to avoid pain, get through the season you're in, or arrive at the next best thing? Like a cartoon, everything is fuzzy in your peripheral vision as it whooshes past you, and the only thing you have eyes on is the "prize" you've labeled as the trophy to win in life.

It's funny how our minds, bodies, and souls are so intertwined that when one of them eventually screams for help, the others have to pay attention. You have a meltdown, burst into tears, lose your cool on someone, or if you're like me, your body starts to shut down.

Recently, I experienced my body's plea for me to stop and take a break in a way I'll never forget. It was mid-December, and the hustle was on to create an extraordinary season of wonderful Christmas memories. I was parenting on my own for a few weeks while my husband was at another training in a simulator for a new plane he would soon be flying. I was closing on a book deal (for this particular book) while also trying to plan a sweet party for Oliver's first birthday amid all the logistics life was throwing at me.

Before I knew it, I woke up in the middle of the night and realized something was terribly wrong with my body. My eyes felt sunken, my chest was tight, my lungs couldn't fill up with enough air to give me the confidence to go back to sleep. The world was swirling around me, and my head was pounding with pain.

I was home alone with the boys, so I made a game plan for the morning if I still felt this way.

I'll just do the little survival necessities. Do I need to call an ambulance? No. Am I being too dramatic?

The next morning, with a baby on my aching hip, I dialed a few people I trust. Tears welled up in my eyes when one friend told me, "I'm coming over. You need to go see a doctor."

Lying on the exam table, typing a text to friends I knew could handle the baton pass of our everyday life, and honestly just trying to take the next breath—I was terrified. After a few panels and moments of waiting, the doctor came back in.

"COVID positive. Flu positive. I need to check your lungs—I'm afraid it's moved and settled as pneumonia."

A few more tests and minutes went by.

"Yes, it's pneumonia. You'll be out for a few days. Do you need a doctor's note for work?"

I took the deepest breath my body could manage, and as the air came out, so did the tears I had been holding on to.

No, I don't need a doctor's note for work! I am my work! I can't call out sick from my children, as much as I'd like to.

"No, ma'am. About my children—will I need to quarantine?"

"To keep them safe, yes. Is there anyone you could call to step in?"

There was, and I'm so grateful for our village that did.

The next six days seemed so unproductive. I felt like I was frittering away my time and wasting away in bed all week while I quarantined. I did a lot of praying in the moments I couldn't keep my eyes open long enough to read or watch a movie or aimlessly scroll. I prayed frustrated prayers, asking God why He would bench me in life's greatest play of the year. Didn't He know my kids needed me? Didn't He know my work needed me? Didn't He know that Christmas and birthdays and celebrations were around the corner?

He did, of course. And then I had a whispered thought: *Don't you know that I don't need you in order for any of that to happen, but I love it when you do it out of rest?*

I didn't like it, but it made sense. My pride melted away as I lay in bed, palms up and tears streaming down my temples.

I needed a time-out, a pause, but I had been too hurried to see this truth. My mind, body, and soul deserved rest. I believed the lie too long that I needed to earn rest, that I had to do enough before I could rest. In that quiet moment, I was humbled by the truth that we don't work to earn rest; we do our best work out of an overflow of rest.

My world shifted. Being benched and watching the game was no longer frustrating—it became restorative. I got the care I needed, caught up my soul to a place it could love well from, and noticed things about my life I had never noticed before. I experienced deep gratitude that I could stay in bed for six days and my people would take care of my boys—and that my body was designed on purpose to do its healing work through rest.

I noticed smaller gifts, too, like the way the blooms from a bush outside my bedroom window move when a breeze hits, and the way my son hums himself to sleep, which I could only hear because I was finally quiet enough to listen.

There I was—still sick in bed, trying to get a deep breath, coughing every time I inhaled too quickly, sore from my body healing—but I was at peace. I had joy and hope for the days to come, when I would finally be on the other side of my closed bedroom door.

When we are zooming through life, avoiding the obstacles, trying to get to the next exit, always swiveling to catch the balls that are about to be dropped, filling our time with different appointments and celebrations to avoid spending time with our thoughts, we miss out on major opportunities. Opportunities for God to show up in the stillness, in the quiet, in the space in our minds that feels void. It's hard to notice His voice and the joy He gives when we're going so quickly that everything in our peripheral is blurry.

Let's seek God's holy design for both productivity and delight by moving slowly, finding healing, getting curious about questions we've always had, trying something new, seeking to understand why we do things the way we do them, and turning off our phones. The result will be finding joy in the life we have—obstacles and all.

Identify the Rest You Crave

Before some of life's meltdowns taught me about rest and the women who have delicately walked with me through them, I would have told you that rest looked like getting eight hours of sleep and taking a nap when you need to. Hear me, there's nothing wrong with sleep—and it's actually an incredibly large part of rest—but it's not the entirety of rest.

Rest could also look like working on a puzzle, sharing dinner with friends, taking a walk in one of your favorite neighborhoods. It could look like learning a new hobby or putting your phone away for an afternoon.

They're all different answers for different versions of exhaustion, and it's on us to identify what type of rest we need in our circumstances. After all, a nap and a snack might not fix the fatigue you feel if your soul is tired—just like a long walk would be unhelpful if your body was tired. So how do we tell what kind of rest we need? There are many types of rest, so I'm dividing them into three larger categories that we'll address together: mental, physical, and spiritual.

If you're ready to dig deeper into the beauty of true rest, I encourage you to explore the incredible work of Dr. Saundra Dalton-Smith and my dear friend Jess Connolly. Dr. Dalton-Smith's groundbreaking insights in *Sacred Rest* helped me understand the seven types of rest we all need to truly thrive, while Jess's wisdom on living with intentional grace has been a steady encouragement in my own journey, particularly through her book *Tired of Being Tired*. Their words have profoundly impacted me, and I'm confident they'll impact you, too, as you create rhythms of rest in your life.

My Mind Needs Rest

SYMPTOMS OF YOUR MIND BEING WEARY:

- Hard to sort through priorities
- Lack of clarity and discernment
- Overwhelmed by making decisions
- Easily overstimulated by your surroundings
- Zoning out and going into a void

Our brains are like muscles: they can be trained to grow strong, but they can also get tired. It's important that we honor our minds and give them a break when we see warning signs that a dead end is approaching. Let's turn things around while we still have some space to do so.

You might have heard it said, "If the devil cannot make us bad, he will make us busy."[1] When I take a moment to recall all the moments I experienced brain fatigue, my mind was loud, chaotic, and full of noises reminding me of the commitments, the guilt, the calls I needed to make, and the decisions I should have made differently. Of course, when we take a step back, we can see that our minds have many reasons to feel busy, thus putting a burden on our lives we were never meant to carry alone.

Simply recognizing that we're tired doesn't give us the proper language or practical ability to move through what we're experiencing, and many times, mental fatigue is at the core of the other "tired" symptoms we feel. Once I find myself noticing the red flag of tiredness, I backpedal by doing some work I've learned through therapy and wise friends of mine. Here are a few practices that have helped me reenergize my brain and bring it back to a place I can count on.

First, I reverse engineer from that moment to the root of my tiredness. For example, if I put the keys in the refrigerator (yes, this happened), I like to laugh at myself first, and then take a few seconds to recall what in the world happened that day to lead up to that silly event.

I went to bed way too late last night, which caused me to sleep in and miss my alarm, so I woke up in a sprint to do the things to get the boys out the door to preschool. I ate the two bites of leftover scrambled eggs on Oliver's plate, and I didn't properly nourish myself. I scrolled (a lot) today and didn't take many breaks from screens during my workday.

Well, there you have it. Not only did I just analyze what led me to the point of putting my car keys next to the yogurt container, but I answered my own questions and gave myself some pointers and ways to move out of my mental fatigue: get an adequate amount of sleep, plan ahead, nourish my body, delay jumping on social media first thing in the morning, take breaks and even set an alarm if I forget to do so.

With prayer and reflection, I think we hold the answers to a lot of our biggest issues. It's just about creating the space for consideration and humility that frees our minds up to see the opportunity for our lives to be enjoyable instead of constantly feeling like a circus.

My Body Needs Rest

HOW DO YOU KNOW IF YOU'RE PHYSICALLY TIRED?

- Constantly exhausted but having a hard time sleeping
- Frequently stressed and rushed
- Getting sick more often than usual
- Very low motivation

We may notice everything from very moderate to very radical signs that our body needs a break. As women, it's often a badge of honor to push our bodies to their limits. Pride can well up in us when we put off satisfying our hungry stomachs or push forward even when our eyes are tired. For many of us, great healing needs to happen here.

Female bodies carry life, literally and metaphorically. They carry everything from emotions to ideas to future generations. Your body is not only God's masterpiece but His pièce de résistance, God's final touch on His creation. In Genesis 2, He had created the whole universe, but somewhere around verse 20, He tilted His head and didn't find anything or anyone suitable for helping the world as it needed help. So he made woman.

Whenever I remember this, I'm moved. I urge you to place a hand on your heart, take a deep breath, and exhale. In this moment, try to recognize the beauty of your God-created body. Sure, she's not perfect. But she's nothing short of beautiful because she's created in God's image and capable of incredible things.

Do we rest as we believe this? Do we give her, our body, the opportunity to catch a break so we can continue to be a brilliant tool made by our Creator to experience abundant life?

My Soul Needs Rest

HOW DO YOU KNOW IF YOU'RE EMOTIONALLY TIRED—TIRED AT A SOUL-DEEP LEVEL?

- Easily annoyed, lacking patience for people
- Don't have the bandwidth to serve others
- Spiritually dry

I love to learn. Tell me a fun fact, and I'll probably remember it. Play me a song, I'll learn the lyrics. A desire to learn is an admirable trait, but it can start undoing me quickly if I focus on knowing the facts above knowing God and being known by Him. Sometimes I take in so many voices, facts, timelines, and studies that I'm not sure what actually belongs and what doesn't. It gets a little too fuzzy to sort out, so I become overwhelmed and I back away slowly. This version of Rachel is apathetic, and easily annoyed and distracted. If I'm not careful, the "fire" I once had for the Lord will die down into a little ember that needs to be fanned and blown on. But I surely don't have the energy to do so if I'm fighting off soul-level spiritual fatigue.

The first time I found myself in this place, I was ashamed and devastated that I would ever question or doubt my faith. I wondered who would understand me since most of my friends are believers, and I thought, *If I could just borrow a little bit of their faith, it might help bring mine back to what it used to be.*

On a recent Fourth of July, I was burned out on many aspects of life and dreaded showing up to a ministry that I once thought was so fun. I wasn't sure how to pour anything from an empty cup, aware that performance was an easy and unhealthy default for me, and I didn't want to fall back into that method of making it through. "Fake it till you make it" was certainly not for me.

This specific holiday was the sweet interruption I needed to enjoy a cookout, some good company, and fireworks, of course. That's what rest sounded like to me at that moment.

Burgers were eaten, potato salad was served, kids splashed in the pool, and someone brought out sparklers for us to light and wave around.

One person lit a sparkler with a lighter and instructed that person to light the others. So we all put our sparklers into a huddle and made sure the ends met to be lit by the shared flame.

We twirled, danced, wrote letters in the air, and made sure to get a fun picture as a group. Eventually the sparkler fun ended when the crackling flames made their way down the wires, and we continued our party.

The image stuck with me, though: each sparkler lit by the next, borrowing warmth from one to light another for everyone's benefit. This is me too. The moment my soul feels weary, I'm not supposed to muster up something false and present it to the Lord in a formal fashion. Jesus gives us the freedom to come as we are—hurt, hung up on questions, unsure if what He says is true. He yearns to reveal Himself to us in our unbelief. It's up to us to recognize the state of our heart and ask Him to be a part of fanning the flame, with the encouragement and support of the faith of those around us.

Our souls need rest, just like our bodies, just like our minds. They are not exempt from becoming weary and heavy.

In Matthew 11:28-30, Jesus says, "Come to me, all you who are weary and burdened, and I will give you rest. Take my yoke upon you and learn from me, for I am gentle and humble in heart, and you will find rest for your souls. For my yoke is easy and my burden is light" (NIV).

The surest way to find rest for our souls, my friend, is to go to Him, not hide from Him out of shame that we don't meet a standard of belief. He is gentle. He welcomes us with open arms when we return to Him.

Give Yourself a Break

I urge you to be curious about what these different kinds of fatigue look like in your life and how you tend to act and think when you need a break. Addressing the light blinking on your dashboard and catching those first few warning signals can be so helpful before the blaring alarm goes off and you have a system malfunction.

Mental Rest

HANG UP AND HANG OUT

My phone consistently adds a level of stress and anxiety to my life. My reliance on it for connectivity often bamboozles me into thinking that if I spend more time on my phone, I am in the know, invested in others, and furthering my relationships. Don't get me wrong—in some ways, this is true. In most ways, it's not.

Spending time in front of screens has an incredibly negative impact on my brain health. Putting away my phone always feels like the "right" idea, but I'm often stumped by how to make it happen. I noticed a few things that make stepping away from my phone screen seemingly impossible: it has no home other than my pocket or right hand, and glancing at it has become a habit I would need to break. So what if we found a place for our phones to live—specifically a space that's not super easy to access? I've been moved to leave my phone downstairs in our kitchen when I go to bed so I'm not tempted to check it first thing in the morning or stay on it late at night. Or what if we created spaces in our home where phones were not allowed so we could be distraction-free? *Truly* putting away our phones gives our mind the break to find rest. We won't be preoccupied with checking notifications or making sure we're always on our toes, answering messages instantly.

Perhaps the connection I value more than texts and social media is connecting with those in front of me. Devices have their time and place, and communicating with them deserves a piece of the puzzle—but how much? That's for us to determine. When we find the right balance, we'll be one step closer to true rest for our mind.

FIND CLOSURE FOR YOUR STRESS

How often are we putting our brain on the fritz by trying to get out the door, sweat beading, slinging our bag into the passenger seat, and in one quick move, turning on the car, putting it in reverse, and backing down our driveway? Or we hit a few hiccups on the way to a work meeting, take the elevator, walk briskly down the hall, and pull the heavy door open to realize we never even caught our breath? That's a lot of hard work that we sign our mind up for to go from one stressful situation to the next without ever pausing for a moment, calming our mind down, taking a few deep breaths, and seeking "closure for the stress" we just endured.

Let's take a moment to put a mental bookend at the end of the stress before stepping into the next part of our day. That gives us the margin to start fresh instead of stringing one long, tense moment to the next.

One way to find closure for our stress is putting pen to paper. It serves us more than the occasional grocery list that sits on our counter or the to-do list we jot down and tape to the fridge. Our brains take a cognitive pause when we write down our thoughts, whether that looks like creative journaling or brain dumping all the ideas and issues that are swirling around in our mind.

I remember a day when I asked Thomas to take the boys on an adventure so I could have a few hours of quiet. I don't notice how loud a space can be until the noise is hushed. I expected that this time would be restful, but the moment the door closed behind them, the intensity of the quietness felt deafening. Tempted to turn on music or the TV to help hush the ringing in my ears, I felt a gentle prompt to just sit and let the commotion that was somehow coming from nowhere dissolve. And, after a few moments, it did.

Turns out, the clamoring of my mind wasn't begging for more noise but for less.

Sometimes the "noise" looks like actual pandemonium of a household, but it could look like the hustle of your workplace or even the thoughts in your own head adding up quickly to create an orchestra of overwhelm. Mine looks like all three. It's the business, it's the advice I take in from anyone willing to help, it's the self-talk, it's the children, the TV, the stimulation from every angle.

I've found it beyond helpful to design a life that expects noise but also creates moments to defuse it. Here's what this looks like for me:

1. Schedule silence.
2. Take a break from books. (Hello, glad you're at least reading *this* one!)
3. Pause podcasts.
4. Notice what I hear when there's nothing to listen to.

There is so much peace, connection, and joy to be found when we give our minds time to rest.

Physical Rest

A NAP AND A SNACK

In 1 Kings 19, we see Elijah, an A-list prophet, get to the end of himself and ask the Lord to take his life (verse 4). In the next verse, he lies down and goes to sleep. Then an angel wakes him up, provides a snack, and tells him to eat. Elijah eats, then goes back to sleep.

Are you laughing? I am. Poor guy. I relate to him—especially hangry, postpartum Rachel.

This story takes me back to my doctor's appointment a

couple weeks after Maddex was born. I shared with the doctor how hard life was at the moment. Gently, she asked me when the last time I had gotten a good night's sleep was.

Is she kidding? I have a two-week-old.

But she was right. Maybe something wasn't wrong with me—rather, I was just lacking the slumber my body craved.

It's not rocket science. Sometimes we just need to take a nap and eat a snack. Seems like simple girl code, but how generous that God created us to operate best and see the best when we're rested and fed. I wonder if we keep ourselves from seeing a life that's lovely when we're not nourishing our body well to do the incredible things it's been designed to do—and when we're lacking the sleep we need to carry on tomorrow.

ANTICIPATE THE SLOW

I've noticed a pattern in my life and my friends' lives: when things slow down, we tend to rush to get our lives together before things speed up again. Then, once they speed up, our fuel tank is just fumes.

Lately, I've been honoring the slow, using it as a pause to catch my breath. This looks like allowing dishes to sit in the sink for longer than ideal. This looks like sitting down during the boys' nap time rather than "knocking out a few things." This looks like not rushing home but taking the scenic route or scheduling a meal with a friend because I have a free evening.

Slow is luxury. So when I get it, I take it.

Spiritual Rest

SEEK TRUTH

When the world makes us weary, the Word does not. In fact, it's the armor we need for seasons when we feel spiritually depleted (see Ephesians 6:10-20). It gives our mind and heart ways to evangelize to our soul when it's weary—and in other seasons, allows our heart and soul to tend to our mind. Even when you're tired, the Word is not.

Storing the Word in our heart for both sunny and rainy days is a gift we can give our current and future self that I hope we never take for granted.

Here are a few passages I love having on the tip of my tongue when spiritually dry seasons strike:

- Philippians 4:5-7
- Psalm 91:1-6
- Lamentations 3:22-23

BE LOVED AND SERVED

Sometimes serving others is a way out of a rut, but it can also be damaging and exhausting if I'm sitting in a place of spiritual fatigue. In these moments, I need to give myself permission to let others help and serve me rather than isolate myself. In past seasons of spiritual fatigue, this has looked like asking others to pray for me when I don't have words, asking friends what God is showing them when I don't have much to see for myself, and being more confident to ask and receive help with everyday logistics without feeling shame for being "needy."

If we are all members of the same spiritual family, and all of us have different functions (see Romans 12:4-5), then it makes sense that others may carry burdens for us when we're experiencing fragility.

SIT IN GOD'S PRESENCE

Prayer is a two-way conversation, but it's okay if you don't have anything to say. If your soul is tired, you probably don't.

Calling our feelings what they are and telling the Lord the truth of how we feel gives Him the opportunity to do something with our feelings that we couldn't do on our own.

It also reminds us that, thankfully, our feelings can't change what we know to be eternally true. When you're in a funk, it's important to remember that our funks only have authority over the world we see and cannot redefine God or change who He is. How refreshing. Although our physical bodies get tired and fail us in some seasons, it's important to remember that there is movement in a world beyond the one we can see—shifts happen spiritually, too, even when we don't feel the quake of them right away. This leads us to a place of soul rest and healing, and it gives us a moment for our heart to catch its breath when we feel fatigued. God's Word is reliable no matter how we're feeling, and sometimes slowing down and sitting in the Truth is the only thing that will restore my joy.

Dietrich Bonhoeffer wrote, "The richness of the Word of God ought to determine our prayer, not the poverty of our heart."[2] It's beyond true. When we take the time to pray and seek truth in a conversation and relationship with the Lord, He will help us find contentment and joy in the everyday. Prayer is more for us to know Him and learn more about His character, and God loves to show us more of who He is when we pray.

My prayer for the version of me that can feel stuck and irritated at the idea of praying—and for you if you can relate—is that slowing down and praying when things are hard wouldn't feel so offensive. Other people may not have the right answers or next steps, but God is always a trustworthy source of wisdom.

I also pray that we would ask God to help us pray when it feels impossible to focus or rest long enough to hear His voice. When prayer seems like a dead end, let's ask the Lord to "help our unbelief" (see Mark 9:24) and to make Himself known to us in those moments we seek him so desperately.

Another way to rest in God's presence is to refresh our soul with worship music. The lyrics of my favorite worship songs calm my soul and fill in the gap with truth. Music can move us and shift us into a space that might require more energy than we have when we're experiencing spiritual fatigue.

In Psalm 46, we see a God who is present, right beside us, helping His people in crisis, with us in the middle of the chaos. Then He reminds us, "Be still, and know that I am God" (verse 10).

For me, this could look like rescheduling something I had planned, carving out time to be alone, or waking up a few minutes early to spend quiet time alone in my home before the day starts for everyone else.

When we can't slow down long enough to notice what's going well, we probably aren't able to notice the causes of the problems that trip us up every day. Once we notice them, we can move them out of the way to avoid stumbling again.

Going after joy is a fight. It goes against our culture. It calls us to be attentive, resilient, and intentional, often putting in labor and tilling the soil so we can see the fruit and harvest it to share with those around us. To do this well, we must walk in a mindfulness that takes strength, that's sharp enough to reframe situations and choose an eternal mindset. If that's the case, then rest is a requirement.

How to Recognize When You Need Rest (And What to Do About It)

Type of Rest	*Signs You Might Need It*	*Practical Ways to Recharge*
Mental Rest	· Your brain feels like it won't shut off · You forget simple things · Decisions feel overwhelming	· Spend a few minutes meditating on God's Word · Write down your swirling thoughts (a "brain dump") · Take a short break from screens or noise
Physical Rest	· You drag through the day · Your body feels heavy or tense · Sleep doesn't seem to help	· Eat nourishing foods · Go for a gentle walk or stretch · Set an earlier bedtime for one night
Spiritual Rest	· You feel out of sync with God · You question your purpose · It's hard to find hope in challenges	· Spend time in prayer and reflection · Listen to worship music · Read Scripture that encourages your heart

CHAPTER 6

JOY TAKES A VILLAGE—LITERALLY

Each of you should use whatever gift you have received to serve others, as faithful stewards of God's grace in its various forms.

1 PETER 4:10, NIV

"Wait! Did you see them?!"

"Who?"

"The cute couple walking their dog up there!" I said on the edge of the passenger seat, with Thomas driving and Maddex in the back.

We had been in Oklahoma for four months at this point, and I had just as many friends as I had favorite coffee shops in our new town—maybe one. The other women I'd met left a few weeks after I met them at a park, or they were just visiting their husbands in training but didn't stay for long, or they were female pilots with schedules just as busy as Thomas had himself. I was done being alone, and it was almost as if there were a glow around these potential friends walking through our neighborhood.

"Slow down! I'm rolling down my window!" I announced. I might have just found the answer to my longing for friendship.

"No, absolutely not. I will not be those people—that's creepy!" Thomas laughed.

We drove past them. I let out an audible huff and pouted in my seat.

"Do you know how weird it's going to look for us to pull a U-turn and drive slowly by and roll down the window to talk to these *strangers*?!"

"Freaking weird. I know. That's why I asked you to slow down the first time," I bantered back.

Our tires screeched as Thomas began the turn. I rolled down my window and enthusiastically waved. The couple stared back and slowed their pace, probably asking out of the side of their mouths, "Do we know this chick?"

"Hey! I'm Rachel! Are you here for pilot training?"

Thomas nervously laughed next to me.

"Yes, we're here for the next few weeks!" the wife replied.

"That's great—so are we! We have a dog too! Maybe we could have dinner sometime soon. Can I have your number?" I was basically drooling at this point, envisioning a friend who might possibly "get me" and who could come over for coffee in the mornings. Whether we hung out for a few weeks or became soul sisters for life—it didn't matter to me at that moment. I just knew I needed a friend and was willing to do anything it took to find one . . . obviously.

She read out her number and I traded it for mine while our husbands talked training and pilot-talk. *Taylor from the street,* I typed into my phone. Saved.

"I can't believe we just did that." Thomas exhaled as we drove away.

I just sat back, smiled, and couldn't wait to see what would happen. I knew that I'd never know the outcome if I didn't try.

This particular season of my life was missing joy—including the joy of community—and it was bringing me to a place I'd never been but didn't hate. I was on a desperate hunt to notice the good around me, and slowly, I started seeing it.

I had other incredible friends, but they lived hundreds of miles away. Long-distance friendships are wonderful, but they don't satisfy our need to be known by the people around us. There's a place for all types of friends: long-distance, multigenerational, in a different season of life, etc. But there is something special about friends who live within a ten-minute drive. That's what I missed the most.

My high school or college-aged self would be absolutely mortified that I would stop a vehicle to talk to a stranger and ask her if we could be friends. She would be disgusted by the desperation. My friend Emily likes to remind me that friendship is forged, not found. It takes effort, creativity, and bravery to cultivate the community you're longing for.

Many of us have settled for company, thinking it will

satisfy the craving for deep friendship that we have hidden in our heart. But let's never mistake company for community.

Having friends to walk through life with can be the turning point we need to start delighting in the life we have. They introduce new "good" to us, or they point out the "good" that already existed but was easy for us to miss.

"Taylor from the street," as I affectionately called her for the next few days, agreed to come to dinner at our home. I learned that she was vegetarian—challenge accepted. Over the following weeks, Thomas and I kept in contact with Taylor and her husband. Along with dinner, we went for a walk and even participated in a golf event together.

During this strange season of searching for the good—in friendships and beyond—I discovered two very important factors that change a casual friendship to an active friendship: being a good friend and having a good friend.

Being a Good Friend

There's certainly not a formula to being a good friend, but there is an art to it. It's one of those things that's not always "caught," so it sometimes needs to be "taught." No matter how easily or naturally this comes to you, there are always ways that we can learn, grow, and develop as friends. If we start by becoming friends with Jesus, He will help us discern how to love, serve, and know the friends around us. Friendship is one big treasure hunt with the prize of sharing a lovely life with others.

There's a story in the Bible that puts friendship on epic display. In this story, a man's friends are willing to be majorly inconvenienced to serve him and get him to where he needs to be: at the feet of Jesus. In Mark 2:1-12, we learn that this man is paralyzed. His friends want to help him, so they carry him straight to Jesus. They're not put off by the many obstacles in their way either. A massive crowd surrounded the house where Jesus was. In order to get their friend in there, they had to climb the building, dig a hole in the roof, and lower their friend to the ground so Jesus could heal him.

This particular story gives us three tangible examples of what a good friend is willing to do—and I took notes so I could share them with you.

Go Out of Your Way

These friends carrying the paralyzed man to Jesus didn't let inconveniences get in the way of showing up and helping meet their friend's needs. For us, this probably won't look like digging a hole through a roof, but it could surely look like surprising and delighting our friends, finding ways to pursue them, and helping them through hard times, even if it's untimely and inopportune for us.

Text your friend when she comes to mind. When you say you'll pray for her, consider actually praying in that moment or leaving a prayerful voice message. Is there an important day for your friend coming up—her due date, birthday, or anniversary of loss? Add these days to your calendar and mark the occasion with her, whether by text or in person. Be a noticer of her likes, dislikes, and quirks. Ask her what her favorite meal is at your go-to fast-food restaurant, and tuck it away for a rainy day. Do you know her coffee order so you can surprise her on a hard day?

Look, I'm no expert—and, in fact, most of these ideas came from the incredible women who surround me and set clear standards for what it looks like to be a good friend. I'm constantly inspired by them. I'll never forget when my friend Madison sent my favorite acai bowl to my front door the morning after Thomas was shipped off to military training or the time Abby brought me a "Congratulations" balloon when I hit a major work goal. There was also the time when Carla stopped everything to come over and help me fold laundry—and brought groceries to cook my family dinner too.

Make a Fool of Yourself (When Needed)

These men who lowered their friend to Jesus did so in front of an audience, but that didn't stop them. The looks, the confusion, the remarks, the judgment were no match for the dedication these men had to seek healing for their friend. For us, maybe that looks like doing the embarrassing thing and standing up for your friend when others are talking badly of her. It may mean celebrating her even if she's in a season where you desire to be, whether in career, marriage, or motherhood.

The world tells us that friendship is fueled by gossip,

happy hour, and a good sale, but there's something much more eternal and fundamental to friendship—faithfulness. Even when relationships get sticky, harsh words are said, feelings get frazzled, or we feel threatened by our friend's success, there is so much value to be found in friends who consider each other above themselves and are willing to be socially inconvenienced for their friend's sake.

Carry Your Friend

Not only did these men deal with the logistics of bringing their friend before Jesus and facing the judgment of the crowd, they also literally carried their friend. Let's not forget the strength it took to transport the man on a mat through town, lift him to the top of the house, and gently lower him to the ground.

This raises questions: Are we willing to carry our friends with the strength we have? Are we praying with and for our friends and lowering them to the feet of Jesus? Are we reminding them of the truth when they feel unequipped, discouraged, or tempted?

In many cases, being a quality friend to others can result in friendships that bring joy, purpose, and delight to our everyday lives.

Having Good Friends

It's easy for us—especially as women—to hear the story of the man on the mat and believe it to be a one-sided story about the importance of "serving people well" and bringing our friends to Jesus' feet. Oh, but there's so much more, my friend. Let's not miss another angle: the mat is for you too.

There are times in our life when we're weary, can't think straight, or fall into the trap of discontentment, thinking our lives don't measure up and therefore aren't "good enough." If that's you, it's time for you to get on the mat and be carried into Jesus' presence, and I pray you seek out the strength of the people in your squad to do so.

You are both sides of the story.

Not all friends are going to be our greatest friends of all time and stand in the gap for us in our most difficult circumstances, but I often overlook the people who are already on my side because I'm keeping my eye out for the "perfect BFF" to hop out from behind a corner.

Having people in my life means I need to drop the expectations of how old they might be, what they like to do in their free time, how they vote, or what season of life they're in and focus on finding loving people whom I can trust to be a part of my life. These, I remind myself, are the real "qualifications" for a friendship: someone who will help you, love you, laugh with you, pray for you, and be the strength to help you stand.

I have friends I'd invite over for coffee who would listen rather than talk.

There are friends who have held my baby while I cried and let out some intense feelings and lies I was believing.

There are friends built for impromptu girls' nights and friends I'd travel the world with.

But there are only a few who would be all of the above.

And that's okay.

The idea that there's a Monica to your Rachel, Lilly to your Mia Thermopolis, or Jess to your Cece is a romantic idea of friendship that doesn't encompass everything a friend could be. I resent the idea that if our connection with a friend's bond isn't like one of these, the need for their friendship is any less.

Let's stop ranking our friendships in a hierarchy and put them on a spectrum instead. This will show us that different friends have different roles in our lives, but they're all valuable gifts from the Lord! We may not be able to rely on the coworker we ride the elevator with every weekday morning to carry the drama from our family the weekend before, but we can be thankful she's always there to chat and start our day on the right note. Let's not be so exclusive about our friendships that no one is good enough to make the cut.

Four Types of Friends

Thomas and I were first-time homeowners in a cute little bungalow in a charming, historic neighborhood, and we were thrilled. We spent weeks decorating, planting herbs, and making our first grown-up furniture purchases, and we really felt in a groove with a few years of marriage and many moves under our belt.

One day, I took the familiar drive home from a workout class, turned onto our street, and saw a red minivan parked in our driveway.

Hmm, that's strange. I wasn't expecting anyone.

Out of an abundance of caution, I dialed Thomas and asked him, "We're not expecting anyone today, are we? Because there's a car parked in our driveway."

Alarmed, Thomas told me to keep him on the phone while I unlocked the front door and stepped inside.

I wasn't sure what I was going to find in our house that would explain why someone was parked there. A friend? A fluke?

As I took the three steps up to my front door, I heard a few women talking inside. What I did next, I couldn't control. I moved quickly, one hand on the handle, the other unlocking the door with my keys. I swung the door open to see about six women in my home, all wearing matching yellow collared shirts.

They looked surprised to see me.

I was surprised to see them.

They looked surprised that I was surprised.

Again, my body took over and words flew out of my mouth before I realized what was happening.

"What are you doing in my home?!"

Thomas was still on the phone pressed between my ear and my shoulder. I realized he was terrified, but I had no way of explaining who was in our house or why they were there.

"We're your house cleaners!" one of them piped up.

My eyes darted left and right following the grain on the hardwood floor, as if this would untangle my confusion.

I turned back to Thomas on the phone. "Did you hire house cleaners?" We couldn't afford it, so I would have been shocked, but part of me hoped he'd say yes just to solve the mystery.

"Nope," he said matter-of-factly.

We spent the next fifteen minutes in my living room trying to figure out why the cleaners were there, how they had a key to my home, and why we were all so confused. Turns out, these women had been coming to my home for months without either Thomas or me knowing. The previous owners had a subscription to a cleaning service that they had forgotten to cancel, and the silly new homeowners (that's us) forgot to change the locks.

We all nervously laughed as the group of women walked single file out the door, broomsticks and vacuums in hand. My floors were half mopped and the linens had been stripped from the bed. They hadn't finished their job—and in hindsight, maybe I should've pretended they were supposed to be there the whole time!

Here's the thing: these women weren't "not allowed" in my home; they just hadn't been invited in. I didn't know them well enough to give them a key.

The point of this story is that we should give some friends access to the deeper places of our life in order for our friendship to flourish, while other friends haven't earned that invitation yet (and maybe they never will).

We have room—and the need—for all types of people and friendships. It can be helpful to understand the role various friends play in our lives (and the role we play in theirs!). Most of our friends can fit into one of four categories: front-yard friends, living-room friends, kitchen friends, and attic friends.

Front-Yard Friends

These are the friends who drop by from time to time. You see them outside, and perhaps they don't even know what the inside of your home looks like. But they don't need to! You care for them even if you don't know them deeply. These are friends you see at work or school. They have a place in your life, but they don't know what life looks like inside your four walls. And that's okay.

Living-Room Friends

These friends get a different type of access: you invite them inside to hang out and stay awhile, maybe play a board game or watch a movie together. These are the friends who know enough about your life to keep up in general conversations, but deeper conversations don't necessarily happen here. Lysa TerKeurst says there's a difference between secrecy and privacy.[1] Secrecy is keeping information from someone to protect yourself and your appearance, while privacy is keeping information from someone to protect others and prevent misunderstandings. A certain amount of privacy is healthy with "living-room friends." Since you don't share an intimate level of friendship, boundaries provide protection in conversation and character. Without the full context of each other's lives, it would be difficult to fully speak into each other's circumstances.

Kitchen Friends

Imagine those friends who stay for dinner, help you clean up afterward, and chat for a while in the kitchen once everything is put away. These are our "kitchen friends." They are friends you'd be able to share hard life decisions with or ask to pray about a difficult situation. They are eager to help you whenever you need them—and vice versa. These friends remind you of the truth, keep you accountable for who you are, and understand the ecosystem of your life.

Attic Friends

Imagine asking for help to sort through the decorations in your attic or the junk in your garage. Is yours as terrible as ours? Scattered? Cluttered? If someone took a picture of these spaces inside my home and posted them online for the world to see, I'd get a little warm in the cheeks. Everyone has these spaces in their homes, right? The same goes for our lives and our hearts.

Only our closest, most trusted friends are invited into these spaces. These are the friends we can cry with. They know the ins and outs of how we think. They often finish our sentences and laugh at that inappropriate thing with us because they know we'd "just get it." They can help us carry our burdens to the cross and organize our thoughts and feelings.

This is a precious place. A really sacred place. This is a place that has to be earned. Someone doesn't just go from being a front-yard friend to an attic friend. Trust must be built over time. These are the friends who will exhort you, encourage you, and pray for you.

As you look at the list above, remember that we need all these types of friends in our lives. We can't truly experience the abundance of life with just one and not the others.

It takes the risky conversation and bravery to introduce yourself to the front-yard friend.

It takes the laughter and "Oh, no way! I had no idea" conversations with the living-room friends.

It takes the clunkiness of learning to do life together with the kitchen friend.

It takes the deep sighs and tears that follow with the attic friend.

Pursue Friendship

There's a chance you're sitting in this moment with a bit of envy for the friendships others have (and a bit of guilt about the envy). Keep doing the work and being a good friend to others. The type of friend you are will attract the types of friends you want. Sometimes friendships will just "click" and happen. But most of the time, friendship will take intentionality, courage, and consistency. All routes to companionship with others are beautiful.

As you reflect on the friendships in your own life, consider the following questions.

1. Who are your attic friends—the people you'd trust with a key to your home? How can you show appreciation for these friends this week?
2. Who are some friends having a hard time? How could you show up for them and encourage them?
3. Think of a friend who's been hard to connect with lately. How can you reach out to her and deepen your friendship with her?

You want to know the difference between my best and worst days? It was having friends to walk through them with me.

I'm convinced that one of the only feelings worse than being wedged in a part of life you don't love is being stuck there alone—and no one has a clue that you're frozen.

There's a list on my phone of people I can call, voice message, and ask to show up for me when I need some help pulling myself out of a rut. I used to be convinced that other people had too much on their plate to help me with my issues and that my inconvenience would threaten our friendship, but now I know I was wrong.

"I would have loved to be a part of that with you," most of my friends and husband countered when I finally chose to open up about how I was feeling about a few aspects of my life.

Something about their response tripped a wire in my heart, and I couldn't help but release all the feelings and overflow of frustration. That's what I needed—just someone to be a part of the hard things *with* me. The next time I found myself in an "ehh" sort of space, you better believe I called on those people—I was holding them to it.

If you wish you had a group of people to lean on and you feel lonely, take heart. I believe that all of us can pursue access to wise friends, especially for moments like these. Because what is hidden is difficult to heal. And it's easier for us to keep things hidden and tucked away when we don't have a safe space to bring them.

This will also be my caveat for finding help through therapy and counseling with a licensed professional. My dad would often joke, "You're either in counseling or in denial," and I know this to be true for myself even today. It doesn't take a crisis to benefit from counseling.

Whether you ask a wise friend you trust to hold the pieces of your life with you or seek a professional to meet with on a regular basis, it is helpful to have someone to work through delicate areas of life with—and someone who points you toward joy.

I'm an external processor, so if I talk long enough about something, I eventually end up at the place I need to be. All I really need is a space to open up about something to realize it may not be as big of a deal as I thought it was. This is not to minimize my feelings and what I'm experiencing, but it helps bring clarity and perspective to what I'm working through.

A friend you trust can lead you to that place of clarity much faster than you can get there yourself. And you can do that for your friends when they're the ones in need.

The best example we have of a good friend is Jesus. Yes, we see Him healing people, serving His disciples, and leading important conversations, but my favorite part of Jesus as a friend was how He shared life with His friends. He stood with them, sat with them, ate with them, cried with them, and walked with them because He knew that His presence with them was more important than all the things He did for them.

How beautiful is that? We were built to model our lives on Jesus': to pursue companionship, to do life together, to have one another, to borrow each other's hope, and to remind one another of truth. Don't do life alone. Dare to know and be known.

CHAPTER 7

MAKING FUN OUT OF THE MUNDANE

I remain confident of this: I will see the goodness of the LORD in the land of the living. Wait for the LORD; be strong and take heart and wait for the LORD.

PSALM 27:13-14, NIV

This counseling appointment came at a great time in the week. I felt like I had done everything I needed to do yet nothing I needed to do all at the same time. Appointments were rescheduled, a babysitter was booked for date night but then date night had to be canceled because something came up or someone got sick—I can't remember. I had to keep too many plates in the air, and before I knew it, the beautiful things I love being able to spin and twirl around in my life (my family, my dreamy job, the love of my life, my home, my friendships) quickly became to-do list tasks to be checked off because I wasn't sure who needed what from me most.

That morning, the elevator dinged, I nodded to the man

I shared the several-story ride up with (he had no idea what was going on in my life), and turned left to head to my therapist's office.

"Hey, Rachel. Come on in."

Before my tush could sit on her sofa, I was making jokes about how hard it was to get to her office that morning because of the traffic and apologizing for the leftover oatmeal breakfast I had on my top from picking up babies halfway through their meal. She asked me how I was doing, but she didn't need to—she knew.

I rambled for a few moments about all my plates in the air and "How do I know which one to put down?" and thoughts like "And what if one drops and breaks?" and more questions and reflections about how to balance it all in life.

"These are beautiful things I'm talking about, and I love them. I'm just starting to"—I shrugged—"resent them?"

She grinned, then responded, "When was the last time you played?"

It was like she found the tenderest place in my heart and gave it a hug. I began to cry.

I wanted to play, I wanted to enjoy life, I wanted to laugh and have fun, and I was even jealous of the people who "had the time" to do it. But wouldn't it be irresponsible of me just to set down all these things in life that "must be taken seriously" in order to play? It sounded like exactly what I needed but also the silliest route to take.

During the next forty-five minutes of our session, though, I started to see things through a different lens. I'd come through the door thinking play would be a bit naive, reckless, and immature. *How ignorant for someone to neglect what's necessary to deal with by playing and having fun.* As a result of this enlightening conversation with my therapist, though, I began to see play as necessary, sophisticated, and strategic—especially when life is begging for a break.

If I'm already overwhelmed and beginning to dislike areas of my likable life, what do I have to lose?

So I decided to give it a try.

I think it's part of human nature to try to fix things ourselves, hide the hard stuff, and brush challenges under the rug. Shove the scary in the closet and hope it doesn't find its way to the doorknob. Whenever another problem pops up for us to solve, we groan, grit our teeth, and grin. It's how we're wired—we know it best.

But perhaps trying to solve everything and dive for each plate before it shattered on the ground was keeping me just busy enough to align with the enemy's desires for my life. Perhaps I was so distracted by what's "good" from the outside looking in that I wasn't experiencing joy from the inside looking out. Rachel needs fun. You do too.

What Counts as Fun

We've been sold a counterfeit. Who's to blame? I'm not sure. But let's trade it for truth when it comes to fun.

Counterfeit: In order to have fun, you have to enjoy every part of your life.

Truth: Being happy and liking everything about your life all the time is not a prerequisite to having fun.

In fact, it's when we have a hard time enjoying our lives and seeing God show up that fun must become a priority for us.

Having fun must not be dependent on how you feel. If that were the case, I would have been disqualified from fun yesterday.

When imagining fun and play, it's easy to picture frolicking through a field of wildflowers, poetically splashing in puddles outside, Princess Mia mattress-surfing down the staircase in the second *Princess Diaries* movie, and so on.

These abrupt interruptions to our life count as "fun," sure. But they are often out of reach and not the realistic, daily kind of play I'm talking about. Perhaps play seems unattainable because we believe it has to be dramatic, time-consuming, and picturesque. Perhaps it's easier than we think it is.

Clean slate. Cut the fluff. What counts as play?

Here's my definition: anything that is truly fun to you, has no real purpose, yet it's intentional.

You have to volunteer to do it.

It has to be something you actually *enjoy*.

You can't be watching the clock.

When you're actually having fun, you often aren't aware of yourself.

It gives you the freedom to ad-lib, pivot, and change your mind.

When something is fun, you'll want to do it again.

My therapist was right, and you may be coming to terms with this too. I hadn't *truly* played in a while.

The more we seek out opportunities for fun and play, the more we'll integrate it into what we're already doing. This shapes our brain to be on the constant lookout for future ways to pursue play. It will become easier to notice the spots in our scheduled pages and planners where play may be possible.

Silly? Irresponsible? Naive? It's easy for my brain to be bungeed back to those thoughts, but then I remind myself that I've been created and wired to do fun really well. It's in my nature; it's who God made me to be. It's how He designed our brains by giving us the gift of endorphins, the feel-good chemical to fight against pain and stress and usher in healing and enjoyment.

Yes! I want more of that!

One of the best stimulants to more endorphins and our brain functioning and firing on all cylinders as it's designed to? Playing hard and having fun.

Fun and play awaken our senses to see where God is and what a good gift giver He is. The invitation is evident: we can put His joy on display.

I want to like the life I'm living, to readily see the availability of abundance, but I'm quick to shrug off the perceived foolishness of actually having a good time and playing. Well, my friend, if you're at the same crossroads I was that day at therapy, the direction you go is a decision you'll have to make.

Doing dishes, going to work, keeping up with my home, sending emails, serving at church, and other mundane tasks that dominate our days may not be inherently fun—but they have the potential to be. It's up to us.

Notice the Fun That Already Exists

Reverse engineering the idea of play was really what helped this habit of finding fun click for me. Lord knew that when I first shook hands with the idea of leaning in and enjoying my life, I didn't have a grand awakening that led me to make any major changes. Actually, I know myself well enough to understand that if I had gone big, I would have gone home and probably wouldn't have tried again.

When it's time for paradigm shifts and cerebrum clean-outs, my tendency is to ditch the whole process, burn everything to the ground, and start again. Intense, I know. Thankfully, I've learned to resist that tendency for the most part. I've learned that the best way to honor myself and the process is to chip away the unhelpful parts and add what's needed little by little.

It had to start small. It had to be the one-degree difference I believed in. So instead of trying to create something fun out of nothing, I just started making do with what I already had and began to notice what was already in front of me. This looked like turning on jazz when I was making dinner and the kids were occupied. This looked like using a mug that made me happy no matter how "tacky" or "extra" it was to anyone else. It looked like choosing smiley face socks that would stick out of my shoes even though I'm in my thirties and everything in the sock section of the superstore was neutral.

When the shift happens and we realize we don't have to craft up fun and joy out of thin air, we begin to see that it's already happening around us. We just have to jump in.

What if we believed the truth that fun already exists, whether we make it happen or not? We are not responsible, nor are we the creators of the beauty or the pleasure to be found in this life.

We don't have to start anything that isn't already happening. We can just jump right into it. The pressure is off for us to perform the right way, tilt our head at just the right angle, pray fervently enough, or check off all the Christian boxes in order to see the fun that exists before us.

Realizing this changes how you see things. Fun is stepping to the beat of the music playing from the restaurant you're walking by. It's noticing and delighting in the hydrangeas blooming on your drive home. It's sitting down to enjoy your meal instead of standing at your counter to quickly eat it. It's smiling at the person walking or driving past you just because. It's the kindness when the person helping bag your groceries genuinely asks how your day was and you lean into honesty. It's the way a thrifted frame with a finger painting from a little in your life can seem so elegant sitting on your nightstand.

The world wants us to believe happiness requires a new purchase, a planned vacation, a fresh bouquet of roses, a date night, new furniture, a new car, or a job promotion. But it's often the familiar that's been written off as "boring" and "humdrum" that puts fun and joy in motion.

Seeing what's right in front of us is sometimes the trickiest thing to do when we're convinced that what's up ahead is more worthy of our attention than the present. What good things has God shown us today that we may have missed because our gaze is directed elsewhere? The present is where we see His presence—and where God is, there is the absolute fullness of joy: "You make known to me the path of life; in your presence there is fullness of joy; at your right hand are pleasures forevermore" (Psalm 16:11).

This tendency to miss what God is doing reminds me of the story in the book of Exodus after the Israelites had escaped from slavery in Egypt. They were beyond peeved with their leader, Moses, when they found themselves wandering in the wilderness, hungry. Moses had cast a vision for them, told them that where they were going was better than where they were. It was the Promised Land, flowing with milk and honey! But their complaining and grumbling was louder than God's promises for what was next (see Exodus 16:2-3).

God was beyond kind to His people and dropped manna—literal bread—from the sky every day for forty years to keep them satisfied. The sweet, flaky white bread was evidence that God was near and would give His people everything they needed in that moment and beyond. The tricky part about the manna was that it came with an expiration date and didn't last beyond the twenty-four hours after it had dropped out of the sky. It was proof that God provided what the people needed that day and a reminder that He would continue to do so in the future (see Exodus 16:14-19).

God's in the business of giving us the evidence, the goodness, the satisfaction we need even when we're hungry, lost, or in a desert season. Let the manna for the Israelites raise the question for us: What manna that we need today has God been dropping out of thin air, covering the ground before us? It didn't do Moses and his followers any good to keep the manna on the ground and continue to protest the life they were living. It won't do us any good either.

Make Normal Things Fun

The "fun muscle" is just like any other muscle: it has to be worked, stretched, and cared for in order to strengthen. I like to think of noticing what's around us as the first step of this workout routine, though it's not the only step. Noticing the possibilities for fun already present in our lives—and making the most of them—is a great way to find joy in our everyday moments.

It can seem so distracting to live a life where you have to be constantly on the hunt for fun—exhausting, even. And sure, while there's good in seeing what's naturally around us that can add a little pep to our step, it's also a crucial part of the equation that we steward what doesn't seem fun at first glance and give it a chance to be a source of joy too.

The normal thing: doing the dishes. The fun thing: calling a friend while you do this chore.

The normal thing: taking out the trash. The fun thing: making an effort to talk to someone you see outside.

The normal thing: exercising. The fun thing: doing it with friends, trying a new workout class, walking on a new trail. Mix it up.

The normal thing: your commute home. The fun thing: taking a more scenic route, rolling the windows down.

The normal thing: your morning breakfast routine. The fun thing: adding a new ingredient or trying a new creamer instead of sticking with the same old, same old.

The normal thing: grocery shopping. The fun thing: picking up a treat that would honor someone you know. Maybe your friend has had a hard day and you grab some flowers or her favorite soda or snack.

Making the mundane fun and seeing the possibility for joy in the ordinary is an act of worship. It's a way to show honor and gratitude to the Lord, who's the source of fun and joy in our lives. It's deciding to remain confident that the goodness of the Lord is here and available to us, regardless of what our circumstances look like right now.

Are we choosing to notice when things go well, or are we constantly trying to solve our problems?

When we focus on the things of God, the richness of life we can experience with Him, and the goodness He has set in front of us, the other things of this world fall into their proper places.

Shifting our gaze from survival to an opportunity to worship is one of the quickest routes to cleaning the lens through which we see life.

Fun, enjoyment, and play is *here*. Not over there, not in a few weeks, not after the kids' bedtime, not tomorrow morning. It's available here. There is a new level to unlock in the everyday routine of our work, our motherhood journey, our singleness, our dating life, or our marriage. The key to all of this is that you are the only person on this planet who has access to the layer of joy available in your life. Even though we're all different, I found it helpful to surround myself with joyful friends so I could take notes on their approach and see how I might apply similar tactics to my own life.

Can I be one of those friends for you now?

Don't wait for the moments deemed worthy of celebration before celebrating.

It's all worthy. The kid coming home confident about the quiz they took, celebrated. The friend who went on a first date, celebrated. The job promotion, the memory verse, the breakthrough in your relationship, the everyday overlooked moments, hold reasons to celebrate. Celebrating could look like lighting the candles on your favorite cake. It could look like picking up a bouquet of flowers or foraging from the ones growing in your backyard or on the way home from work. Celebrating counts as the hug that lasts a few seconds longer or not waiting for the perfect occasion to use your dinner china. Use the fancy teapot just because. Turn on the dance music and trot around your house. Worship through celebration.

Try doing the thing you've always wanted to do but thought would look silly.

Or maybe you haven't tried it because you're afraid you'd change your mind and have to start over. Having the courage to try something new is the first of the steps of faith that eventually add up to miles of proof that you indeed can do something different. For me, I knew I wanted a green dining room. I craved a more colorful home but worried it would look too bold.

How green does green get, and what if it's so vibrant I have to put in more sweat equity and gallons of primer just to get it back to the creamy white I've been told it should be?

A few trips to the home improvement store, a few swatches, and lots of deep breaths later, I was trying out the greens in my dining room. Before I knew it, I'd chosen one. I painted the whole room and actually didn't hate it! *I can always change my mind, right?*

"This isn't permanent," Thomas gently reminded me.

Painting the dining room was my most recent step of faith, but I started with smaller steps. Before this painting project, I decided to make a new recipe for my friends who'd recently had a baby. And before that, I took a different route home that had speed bumps (because my boys love throwing their hands up over speed bumps). If we followed the trail of steps all the way back to the beginning, we would find something much more ordinary. If you're still taking the first courageous steps, don't worry! You'll work your way up to bigger things quickly. A few weeks ago, I actually added a *patterned wallpaper* to a wall in my dining room. The evidence of pursuing fun is there, and it can be so fun to try new things.

Make a game out of little things.

If you want to see the competitive side of me—the one that laughs so hard I snort or the spicy personality that's too witty to handle sometimes—we should play a game. A board game, a card game, or a "life game"—like who can spend the least amount of time on their phone in the afternoon? Who can I call on my commute and leave a voice message for if they don't answer? How fast can I (safely) unload the dishwasher? Can I memorize the lyrics to the new song I love that's on repeat while I organize my closet or vacuum my house? These simple but super fun games give common tasks a little more delight than if they had been completed in silence, alone, or without any play.

What's in Your Way?

For some of us, making normal things fun doesn't come naturally, and there are hurdles standing in our way that intimidate us when we start to look for joy. I've been there. And I'll probably be there again soon. But I've discovered tools that help me see the obstacles for what they are—frail. One of the best tools: other people. When my boys are with me, I tend to go slower, see more, and lean in a bit more, and this yields memories I'll cherish forever. When my friends are involved in my daily life, our relationship goes to a new level. When my family is involved, I find segues into conversations that allow me to invest more deeply in future generations and learn more about my heritage.

Many times, however, I build up the idea that an obstacle is immovable or too time-consuming to deal with. I imagine this raging game of tug-of-war between me and it, and before I realize it, I'm so entrenched in "overcoming" it that I forget it's already been defeated and it's up to me to drop the rope and walk away. Let me remind you of what Ecclesiastes 1:9 says: "There is nothing new under the sun." This includes your obstacles and your reasons why you shouldn't go for joy by playing more in your life. Some excuses can be louder than the truth: "It would be too difficult to [fill in the blank]." "I'm not the 'host type,' so my house wouldn't be the best to gather at." "This is the way I've always done it, so why change it?" In reality, we are not only worthy of a life we enjoy but called to become so good at joy that it causes others to be curious about the life we live and the Truth we believe.

I wonder how many of us are stuck in that space of being too distracted and paralyzed to try anything new. If we were to name these obstacles and come up with a plan to navigate them, I wonder if we'd realize they are smaller than they seemed. I wonder what would happen if we started to believe that God's Word is a lamp to our feet and a light to our path (see Psalm 119:105) and took the next step that the lamp revealed in order to make our way back to the abundance we know to exist and that we know is *for us*.

Let's name it: What's actually in our way of playing well?

"I don't have time for it."

Actually, you don't *not* have time for it. Fun possibilities already exist in our daily lives, so they're not something we have to create—they're something to notice. Fun can be discovered on our drive from one meeting to another. Joy can be found when we take a few extra seconds to acknowledge the stranger at the grocery store. Fun and joy are integrated into our day—woven throughout—but they're easily missed. Fun isn't something we need to "have time for"—it's something we get to create a margin for. Once we do that, we'll see it in the spaces where we already find ourselves and in the middle of what currently occupies our calendar.

"I just don't feel like it."

Thank God our feelings don't determine the truth. And thank God we've been given the gift of emotions, but it's up to us to make sure we don't allow them to control us through what we believe and how we carry ourselves. To sit in our sorrow for too long can lead us to a deepened sadness we hope to never know. To sit in our anger leads us to resentment, rage, or even apathy, and it becomes hard to see through our current situation. To start *feeling* like enjoying things again begins by getting small tastes of heaven on earth enough for our heart to crave the truth rather than our feelings. Meeting a newborn for the first time, the first scent of fall, the sound of laughter around a campfire, the taste of a warm meal someone else prepared, the soft breeze after a deep breath—these are the moments that I feel the layer between heaven and earth grow thin. You can nod to the hard things without bowing to them. The choice to seek joy even in the midst of pain is brave and bold and possible. The times we don't feel like playing and having fun are often the times we need to most of all.

"What will they think of me?"

I pray we're surrounded by many people who champion the joy of Jesus in our lives rather than those who make us prove it exists in the first place. It's common to live with loud voices that make a case for being "mature" and "polite" rather than having fun—and that's a tough place to be. When you surround yourself with people who hunt for joy in their own lives, you start to see the fun and moments of play infusing your spaces too. These joyful people exist, and their friendship will change your life.

"I'm in an inspiration drought."

Creativity surges and droughts exist. To have to pour the same amount of energy into our lives and the lives of others when we're wearing thin is a mantle too heavy to carry sometimes. I like to think I'm doing myself a favor by literally keeping notes of all the fun I want to have when my energy returns. Here's what that looks like: when I have an idea of something I'd like to make or do or someone I'd like to hang out with, I'll write it down for a future day when it is actually possible. One thought typically leads to another, and before I know it, I have a list of twenty ideas of fun outings and free activities in my area for the summer, rainy days, with the kids, on my own, and everything in between! I then reference it on the days when those ideas come less naturally to me but I know that I need to get out of the house and have some fun and play in life.

What Does This Look Like for Me?

The act and worship of play has led me to more zeal than I knew my life could hold. It has become an overflow and an offering that I now love to include others in as I continue to challenge myself to try the new thing, celebrate where I can, honor those around me, and use the dang teapot because why not?

There are moments surrounding us on a daily, hourly, and second-by-second basis demanding that we "oooh," "ahhh," and "awww," and just as much as I think it's important to see the fun that's right in front of us as well as plan for fun in the future, it's just as important (if not more) to take time and recall what those fun-filled moments have looked like in our past.

What do I enjoy?

Because if I've enjoyed it once, chances are I'll enjoy it again. If it happened once, it may happen again. In honor of giving credit where credit is due, I like to keep a list of practical, everyday things that bring me joy.

Here it is:

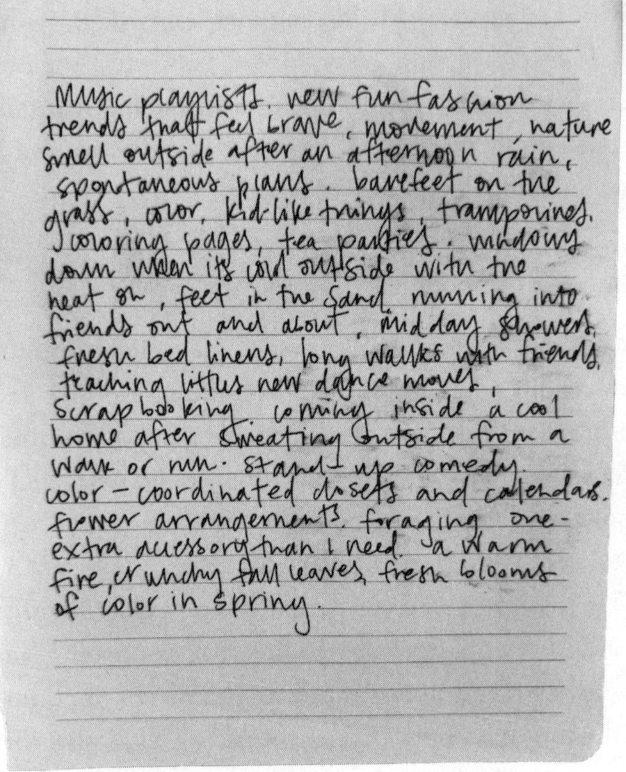

Music playlists. new fun fashion
trends that feel brave, movement, nature
smell outside after an afternoon rain,
spontaneous plans. barefeet on the
grass, color, kid-like things, trampolines.
coloring pages, tea parties. windows
down when its cold outside with the
heat on, feet in the sand, running into
friends out and about, midday showers.
fresh bed linens, long walks with friends,
teaching littles new dance moves,
scrapbooking, coming inside a cool
home after sweating outside from a
walk or run. stand-up comedy.
color-coordinated closets and calendars.
flower arrangements. foraging. one-
extra accessory than I need. a warm
fire, crunchy fall leaves, fresh blooms
of color in spring.

I challenge you to take a moment and do the same. The evidence of joy is all around us in our ordinary lives. The evidence that God cares for us is planted in every step we take—I just don't want you to miss it. He's a good Father who gives good gifts that are ours for the taking!

CHAPTER 8

WHAT LIVING IN A CAMPER TAUGHT ME

Because we loved you so much, we were delighted to share with you not only the gospel of God but our lives as well.

1 THESSALONIANS 2:8, NIV

When Thomas and I first got married, we dreamed of a lively adventure where we got to escape the South where we were raised, even if just for a few months. We began our newlywed escapade when Thomas got a job working for a ministry that would take us to the tip-top of California.

Most families on staff at this ministry didn't live in California year-round but would pack up their belongings and take them in bins across the country to set up a temporary home for the summer. I was always interested in seeing how these families made themselves truly at home in a space that felt so fleeting. A few months there and then back to the other side of the country. It looked chaotic, the logistics were nuts, but somehow I found peace there, thanks to Jen, a woman who would quickly become my friend. Jen had known the ranch for years. Her husband was Thomas's boss, and during the summers the spouses were able to become great friends.

Jen invited me over for tea one afternoon to see how we were adjusting to the pace of this new job and lifestyle that swung back and forth every few months like a pendulum. I had expectations that I'd feel seen and met and loved on, but I hadn't anticipated the other feelings I'd have as soon as I stepped through the door of her cabin tucked inside a forest of redwoods.

A warm smell emanated from a flickering candle on the thrifted table in her entryway. A beautiful cowhide rug that Jen said a friend had passed down to her added the perfect "You're welcome here" vibe. Jen showed me her eclectic mix of mugs to choose from—none of them matched, that I can remember. Family photos were all over this house that Jen and her family had only been in for a few days.

I wonder why she brought all of this from Alabama to California just for a summer.

And despite the cracked paint from the building weathering many seasons and outdated appliances and overgrown ivy on the back deck, it was all . . . lovely.

We enjoyed sipping our tea, although my mug was more full than empty since I was talking more than sipping. I'm still so grateful for the time Jen poured her wisdom and love into me during that experience. Many other women encouraged and welcomed me like this that summer and the few summers we went back afterward: Jen, Edith, Nikki, Mallory, Katie. I remember them well, and I could draw a picture of their homes because they were memorable too. They weren't perfect, but those moments will be ingrained in my mind forever because I exhaled deeply in those spaces. Not because of what these women had but what they did with what they were given.

They made the most of those spaces with their records playing the coziest acoustic songs that pulled out the places in my heart that needed tending.

It was the way they taped pictures to the wall with the cutest washi tape they found at a local art store for the perfect personal touch.

The way they placed the wildflowers that grew on the trails right outside their homes into jars.

The way they used tables and chairs that they had found literally on the side of the road in perfect condition a few days after praying that they'd love a larger table for more people to gather over a meal.

They saw beauty in what was around them and leaned in.

They didn't go far to find what was missing for them. Instead, they looked right where the Lord planted them.

Like I said, it wasn't perfect. But it was peaceful. It held joy.

Luxury maybe isn't the right word, but I felt luxury when I sat in those homes. The richness of the culture that surrounded me, the environment that made space for joy to exist even when hard conversations and tears melted into those sofas. I treasure the wisdom these women unknowingly handed me about creating a home that feels safe for myself and others, that provides respite when we're weary. These days, it's easy for me to find systems and solutions for issues in my home with what I already have because of the resourcefulness I saw in those women. It's easy for me to notice moments worth celebrating, and I have the tools in my home to honor those around me.

These tools aren't only for me and the women who taught them to me. They're for you too. They might seem frivolous, but they're mandatory to create the margin and space in our homes so we can find joy in the midst of lives that sometimes seem unlikable. We can carry that joy as an act of rebellion against anything that counters the idea that life is lovely.

Now I understand exactly why Jen would find a space for those pieces to travel across the country with her—they were meaningful. They held stories that needed to be told in California too. Perhaps we have the same opportunity to make the most of what we have, put seemingly unnecessary items on display, and give the ordinary and mundane a moment to be beautiful too.

An Open Home

I wonder if our homes hold the answers to a lot of the questions we have about why our lives are so hard to like. I wonder if the chaos around us keeps us from experiencing the release we need from the world on the other side of the door. I wonder if we've given too much weight to our reasons why we aren't able to have people over to our homes: *too small, too far away, not beautiful enough, too old, rented.*

I wonder if we're focusing so intensely on the parts of our lives that need fixing and solving that we are missing opportunities for celebrating. And I wonder if we even have the right understanding of what deserves celebrating and how to acknowledge those moments. Making the intention to celebrate in our homes—whether it's popping a bottle of bubbly, lighting candles, or waving sparklers in our driveways—shifts our spaces from being just locations to places of commemoration.

We can have the best intentions of taking steps to create a home that is what we desire it to be for ourselves and others, but if you're like me and my friends, you may feel a bit lost as to how to actually take these steps. We need a plan to follow.

Someone just boss me around and tell me how to do this.

I'm no expert, and I can quickly fall into the trap that adding things to a cart will fill my heart. But allow me to remind both of us of the reasons why loving our home is one of the most important ways to start loving our life and seeing the joy that's right here, available for us.

Some of my best memories and nostalgic moments bring me back to my friends' imperfect homes that were lavished in love. These memories wouldn't exist if I wasn't invited in. I enjoyed the moments, and I laughed way too hard, had conversations that led me to closure or allowed me to rest well.

If we were to copy and paste what my friends did to make their homes so welcoming, I would offer these two steps:

1. Invite people over to your home.
2. Don't apologize for what your home is.

I can't help but think of the story of the sisters Mary and Martha in Luke 10:38-42. They opened their home to Jesus and hosted *God in the flesh* right where they were. I mean, if they weren't intimidated to do that, I don't know why I have such a hard time inviting friends over for an impromptu boxed brownie dessert and card game.

Here's what I want us to see from this story: while Martha was hurried and frazzled, preparing for her home to be perfect (hello, that's me), Mary was simply sitting with Jesus and listening to what He had to say.

Jesus didn't need a perfect home. He just needed an open home.

What a beautiful picture of what is required of us to show hospitality.

What makes an inviting home? Here are some ideas I'd love to share that I keep as a little checklist in my mind.

Is there a place for people to sit and rest? A couch, chairs, table, porch—pillows on the floor, even?

Are you allowing visitors to help you? People feel welcomed when they have some ownership in your home. This may look like accepting their help with folding your laundry, setting the table, cutting veggies while you finish a recipe, drying dishes while you wash—simply doing life with you. Allowing them to meet a need when they're there gives them a sense of belonging and usefulness. Simple but groundbreaking, coming from a girl raised in a Southern culture of "No, I got it—thanks, though!" when I actually do not have it and would love help doing a few things here and there. That's my Martha-ness. We're working on it.

If there is a space of silence, are we leaning into the hush? Are we actually sitting down, listening, being quiet enough, and creating an area where our guests can find what they need through conversation or simple calmness?

When my home feels chaotic or weary, I like to throw on a playlist that shifts the atmosphere. Perhaps that means instrumental jazz (I learned this from my Mimi) or calming worship music or acoustic indie music.

Providing a place of respite for weary souls—ours or someone else's—is a gift our homes carry for all of us, no matter what. There's a benefit for others when they experience the gift of peace in our homes, but it's a gift that makes a difference for us too.

A Place of Order

One thing that highlights the hard in my life: disorder and disarray.

When the mail is scattered over the counter, the bills to pay feel hidden in the pile, and my anxiety starts to creep up my neck.

When the shoes are hard to find, I feel rushed and frustrated, and it brings out the side of a wife and mom that I don't want to default to.

When the bed isn't made, I'm tempted to crawl back in, the room feels more cluttered than it actually is, and I'm annoyed.

God created our life with an order that fascinates me. He cares about structure and routine but also creates space for wonder, mystery, and flexibility. But if there's too much flexibility, my brain aches for some consistency and predictability.

Systems that work for them—or me—may not work for you. That's okay! It's a beautiful thing to know our home well enough to understand what will honor its function and what won't. Take what you need.

Here are a few systems I'll offer up that have tremendously blessed our home.

Decluttering

Many times I realize I've taken in so many objects, products, ideas, and systems without swapping out anything first. Before I know it, my coat closet, garage, and mind are disorganized and pure mayhem. I have a new rule that I try to get rid of something or trade it out before bringing in something new.

If I buy a new item for our home, I consider whether it has a place to live or if I just like the way it looks in the store. Will this take the place of something? Is it an upgrade of something that I can donate or give away?

If I'm trying out a system, I try to consider whether it will actually work for me and improve my family's functionality or whether I'm attempting to meet the standard of someone else's home and the way it functions. For example, organizing my sock drawer—am I doing this because Pinterest told me to or because I actually want my socks to be organized? (It's the first one.) Or does my laundry room have to be cute and organized just so, or will my functional basement situation work? My answer: it will be just fine as is.

Mindfully decluttering my home gives me the clarity and order I need to see the home I have as lovely, enough, and full of potential.

Finding a home for everything

"I can't find the keys—again!"

"Mom, where are the snacks?"

"Do we have any more paper towels?"

Questions like these used to send a shudder down my spine. I felt needed for everything. I was overwhelmed that the people in my home felt little autonomy and relied on me in place of any actual system. Shoes were here, there, and yonder. Cups were shoved in cabinets wherever they fit. Dirty clothes were left at the bottom of the stairs because sometimes the effort to go up them to find the hamper felt like a little too much—that's real.

I can't remember exactly what prompted me, but one day I stepped back and took an overhead look at what was happening in my home. People, including myself, didn't know where to put items, so they easily got lost, misplaced, and replaced—just to find them again, and now we have two of the same thing (me the other week with our kitchen scissors). Can you relate?

Here's the solution that works for my family: everything in our home has a home, and you take it home when you're finished with it. Need a bib every time the baby goes into the high chair? Add it to the back with a Command hook. Looking for sunscreen or bug spray every time you go outside? Try storing it somewhere close to your front or back door. Losing your keys often? Hang them on a hook. Is your underwear drawer stressing you out every time you go to look for your favorite bra or pair of socks? Try shoeboxes to organize it. Shoes scattered everywhere, along with toys or towels or anything else you wish you could contain? Try a basket, with a lid if you can score one. It makes containing and cleaning up easy!

Arranging our time

Order in our home goes beyond finding a way to arrange our things. It also looks like arranging the time we spend in our home. Seeing the way we spend time in our home, like a schedule, can help us become more present in knowing not just *where* something belongs but *when* it belongs too.

Do you have blocks in your time to let your dishes pile up in your sink just like you do for when you do the dishes? Both are lovely. Do you set aside time to play and rest like you do to clean? Both are honorable. Do you make time to sit back and appreciate the parts of your home you love most, or are you constantly on the hunt for how to upgrade? Both have their places when they're balanced appropriately.

We've created a language in our home that allows people to know how to fit into the flow, and it helps guests understand what's going on so they don't feel out of place.

"Help yourselves."

"We were just about to get the boys down for bed—want to join us upstairs?"

Or the infamous "We made too many enchiladas. Does anyone want some leftovers?" message we send to our neighbors' group text.

When we have visitors, there's so much grace for messes to happen. We pray they know that, and we also love the freedom and rest we feel when that permission is granted. There's a time to clean and there's a time to play. Similarly, there's a time to improve and there's a time to appreciate.

I pray we gain a new discernment in our lives to see what belongs when.

Magic in the Mundane

The distraction of things I wish were different can easily keep me from seeing the beauty and likability of what's right in front of me—especially in my home.

I can be so focused on the burp cloths lying everywhere that I forget to be grateful for the children in my home.

I can be so overwhelmed by the dishes sitting on the table from the rowdy night before that I don't appreciate the blessing of a warm meal and a family to share it with.

I have to be intentional in noticing the beauty in the ordinary and the mundane, but when I am, it hushes the loud voices of discontentment.

I've been working on the discipline of finding the magic in the mundane, and it has truly changed the posture of my heart. It allows me to see the beauty in front of me that otherwise is easy to miss. It has become so much easier to accomplish this when I look down at what I'm doing and ask myself, *How will this impact the future of those around me?* Almost immediately, I see ways to pray for other people or other things when going about my various tasks.

Praying over where my children will go that day as I match their socks.

Praying over the purity of their hearts as I fold their little undies or put diapers away.

Praying over the conversations we'll all have at work and school as I prepare lunches or meals.

Praying over peaceful sleep as I rock babies.

Praying over the guests who will sit at my table as I make the coffee for Bible study or set the places at the dinner table.

Praying that God would show up mightily in my marriage as I fluff the blankets and pillows on our bed.

Praying for protection over my home as I lock doors and turn off lights at the end of the day.

These small moments are not just ways that I am petitioning God to show up in my life; they're evidence that He's already here, dwelling in my home. He's adorning every doorframe, cushion, and doorknob. He's here with us in our home now: God with us. He knows all the conversations and arguments that we'll have within these walls, and He is ready to meet us here and bring peace: Jehova Shalom, the Lord is peace. He's healing the parts of our homes that feel unsafe and broken and is making a way for victory: Jehova Nissi, the Lord our victory.

Let's turn to God so we don't lose our footing and stumble over what could be marvelous in our mundane.

Celebrate Small Victories

One of my favorite ways to bring meaning to the mundane in my home is through the power of celebrating. Where better to celebrate than in our homes? When we stop waiting for the perfect moment to celebrate and find ways to champion others who we share our walls with or invite into our space, we create a culture of celebration that becomes the ecosystem that surrounds us and aligns the posture of our hearts and homes with that of joy.

My family and I have begun a habit of celebrating not only when we feel like we have "arrived" or accomplished something but also when God is on the move in the "not yet" and "almost."

We have fun drinks saved in our fridge for minor work wins or parenting days that feel like maybe we are getting somewhere.

There are paper products stashed in a drawer to pull out on a whim when we want to share a store-bought cake with our neighbors in the front yard after something happens that we all want to laugh about (like when our power was restored after days without it from a thunderstorm).

You can find sprinkles in our pantry that we'll dash into pancake mix or add on top of store-bought cookies when we throw a spontaneous party in our home.

A few years ago, if you had asked me how I celebrate, I would have described popping champagne and making reservations at our favorite restaurant.

Now I know it's much simpler. It's using our wedding china on any given Tuesday evening, it's a picnic on the front lawn instead of lunch inside because the weather is nice. It's a handwritten note to say thanks for a coffee date. It's the fresh flowers we pick up for ourselves at the supermarket. It's the "Get Well Soon" balloon we buy for comedic relief because we know life will surely get better soon. It's the water bottles and snacks we leave on our front porch for delivery drivers.

Celebrating small victories boosts the attention we give to the opportunities for joy around us. Joy will overflow naturally as we choose to delight in everyday moments. Celebrating is a declaration of what our home *will be* and what our home *will hold*, regardless of the circumstances and conversations happening in and outside of it right now.

There's power in the way we observe what's lovely in our lives. It starves the discontentment that can sneakily enter through the cracks in our walls and adds roots to our foundations.

The Power of Hospitality

Opening up our home is not only encouraged—it's required. It shifts the focus from *What can my home offer me?* to *What can this home be for others?* In hospitality we find freedom because our gaze is no longer on our brokenness but on the life we have access to through community and conversations.

But I can't cook. I don't have matching dishes. My home isn't big enough. I don't know what we'd talk about.

There's a big difference between hospitality and entertainment. Entertainment is "Throw everything in the closet! Make sure the floors are vacuumed!" when you're hosting a party. Hospitality is plainly sharing your life with others. The pressure to entertain people will lift when you realize that hospitality is simply saying yes when someone knocks on the door of your home. It's texting "Do you want some coffee?" and brewing a little bit more for your neighbor to come over.

If your life is filled with studying for an exam or meeting work deadlines, invite someone over to sit with you, help you study, or bring a treat for a conversational break. This is hospitality.

If your life is lonely and you don't share your home with anyone at the moment, invite over a friend each week to watch the show you've both been loving and looking forward to. This is hospitality.

If your life is filled with littles and babies and you want some adult dialogue but need help folding the laundry or putting your kids down, invite over a friend in a different season of life to help you. This is hospitality.

We've opened up our home to college students who are hungry but in a hurry. We have to-go containers to fill with warm food, and we meet them at the door so they can swing by, dine and dash, or stay for a while if they need to catch their breath.

I've left the front door unlocked to trusted people who need a quiet space to pray and get away for an afternoon.

I've invited some moms to drop their kids off while they run an errand they'd rather do alone.

We've quickly done up our guest room for a friend who was driving through, put on a pot of coffee or tea for a friend who needed a listening ear, and created a space to love on those who needed support and help in tangible ways.

And others have done the same for us.

It's so easy to overcomplicate hospitality, which makes it seem much harder than it actually is. Overcomplicated hospitality is intimidating, and before we know it, we suffer from perfection paralysis and can't make any move at all. True hospitality gently interrupts our loneliness, our overwhelm, and our perfectionism, leaving us with a desire for community, service, and purpose—all of which will greatly enhance the likability of our lives.

A Gathering Place

Saying yes to company and community is much easier when you feel prepared. When we put things in place to make hospitality simpler, it becomes a natural rhythm of life. I know this to be true for my family.

During our military training journey, I often found myself twiddling my thumbs or helping my husband study his flash cards while longing for a sense of community. I envied the camaraderie that existed outside of our home among all the men and women who wore flight suits.

Surely there's a way for me to be a part of this.

The life I had was enough, but I couldn't help noticing the distinction between the community of pilots and the lives that we spouses lived.

There's got to be a way to blend these two groups, to encourage the people around here to gather, connect, grow, and be a part of this picture together.

I just had to find it. This started the hunt for how to make it easier for me to invite people over and simpler for them to accept the invitation.

It started with a night where I made boxed brownies—nothing fancy. As I cleaned up dinner, the pilots studied in our living room on lawn chairs, the floor, and our sofa while their binders, papers, and protractors were spread across the floor and nothing but crumbs were left on the plate of brownies I had set on the coffee table.

The success of this night gave me the confidence I needed

to try it again. This time, I made a few other plates of snack-type foods. The crowd got bigger.

I saw the need for disposable plates when I realized, *Maybe ditching the platters would make this easier for the crowd.* It did.

Water bottles, paper plates, break-and-bake cookies, store-bought chips and guacamole—easy.

It wasn't perfect and it wasn't impressive, but it was exactly what everyone needed: a sense of home, a place to gather and rest in the midst of an intense training season.

Before I knew it, we started making friends, inviting people to church with us, and running into these familiar faces at the commissary and other places on base. Friendships were made, spouses connected, and new plans began to happen: movie nights, game nights, and craft nights with the spouses while the pilots in training studied. A true win-win.

This turned into a weekly meetup, and it gave me the confidence, the tools, and the mental checklist to copy and paste for gatherings in the future.

Bible studies.

Small groups.

Girls' nights.

Playdates.

These gatherings are different in many ways, but hosting them looks similar. They just require something to drink, something to snack on, an easy way for guests to serve themselves if needed, music in the background to fill the silence so people don't feel anxious about conversation, basic supplies depending on the occasion (baby toys, pens, paper), coffee (almost always necessary), and a place to meet.

Hospitality doesn't have to be artisanal meals, beautiful heirloom platters, and freshly mopped floors—although there's nothing wrong with those.

Hospitality is being brave enough to show up and being willing to go first in creating a space where others can show up and experience joy too.

One Hundred Square Feet of Joy

Those three months we lived in a camper in California were some of the best months we've had. The camper was from the eighties, and you could tell. It was funky and retro and outdated, with three small steps that led up to a loft bed and a stall shower that made it tricky to keep my hair clean and shampooed. But, inspired by Jen, I was determined to make it home for us.

After a few trips to a bargain store for contact paper, spray paint, and Command hooks, it was "ours."

We added a faux backsplash of patterned contact paper that was intended to line drawers, but I liked the pattern enough to use it in our mini kitchen. We threw blankets over the upholstery, framed some wedding pictures, and laid a "Welcome Home" doormat right outside.

That summer, we squeezed five people around our drop-down kitchen table booth for a game of cards and Yahtzee, snuggled and read on the petite sofa, strung lights outside, and sat in lawn chairs to debrief our days and weeks. It wasn't perfect, but it was charming. The friends who gathered, the atmosphere built up of laughter and storytelling, the smell of the pines, and the squeak of the door brought life to our space in a way that extra square footage never could have done.

The summer went by, and it was time to return the camper and move home to our first apartment in Alabama. Once the camper was lugged away, just a dead patch of grass was left. Thomas walked toward it, turned back, and smiled.

"I wonder how big that actually was." We hadn't gotten a measurement yet.

He stepped it out, measured loosely, spun around, and laughed. "One hundred square feet!"

One hundred square feet. Three months. Many memories, innovative decorating, newlywed arguments, and laughs. Precious.

Friend, every home has limitations. But those limitations don't have the power to determine how creative you can be with what you have, how often friends gather in your space, or how much love and encouragement you can pour out on the community that gathers there. Within your own walls, there's potential for so much joy and a life you love.

These days, our home looks very different. But I'm still finding very similar joys.

Here are just a few ways I find joy in my home: noticing how the light comes in our window around nine in the morning and making sure I bask in the sunshine for a moment. It melts away tension I didn't know I was holding. The blue-and-white vintage mug that I tend to use on days I feel inspired and the larger pink mug with flowers that my friend gifted me on days when I need an extra few ounces of coffee. Our green dining room, which blesses me with the greeting of color and peace every time I walk in the door. The baskets scattered around my house to catch the clutter that otherwise would be on the floor. Even the toys and hooded towels strewn across the floors in bedrooms and bathrooms upstairs bring a grin to my face when I see the evidence of joy in my boys' childhood. The shade underneath the crape myrtles in our front yard that have been the shelter for conversations with neighbors who have quickly become friends. The way those trees bloom mid-June every year with a sprinkle of pink. The thoughtful handwritten notes that I hung on the wall in the antique frames I picked up at a thrift store the other week—I love seeing these notes, especially when I feel lonely.

Where do you notice joy and abundance in your home? Is it in the places you often overlook or take for granted, like the view out the windows? Is it the tiny touches and imperfections that come from stories and add character, like the crayon drawing on the wall that you could either scrub off or frame? Maybe it's the culture you're creating in the walls of your space: sacred, peaceful, hospitable, holy. Or perhaps it's all of the above.

CHAPTER 9

THIS LIFE IS YOURS FOR THE TAKING

The moment the cursor started blinking and I opened my laptop and created the document that would soon become this book, splinters in my life started to appear, and the loveliness of my life seemed to be dissolving in front of me. My husband lost his job, I received earth-shattering news about dear friends, my podcast studio was broken into, our plane was involved in a crash. I'd text my editor and a few others on my publishing team, filling them in on what was new in Rachel's world because it became comical and no longer a surprise. I was writing a book about loving your life even if you don't like it, and truth be told, I started to not like my life very much.

But let me also tell you that so much healing happened for me in these pages. I've been able to reflect on the work God has done in my life, and it's given me a level of peace, resilience, and joy beyond the hurts and hang-ups the past few months have served to me and my family.

I saw the scale from typical to tragic and everything in between up close and personal. I, too, had to choose to believe in truth when my heart felt defeated, when I felt abandoned and unsure if there was anything good around me anymore. I saw the importance of maintaining a village, calling out for help, serving others to keep my eyes off myself, the sacredness of a home, how authentic hospitality is healing, and how rhythms give me the legs to stand on when days are chaotic.

My hope is that you've seen growth within yourself too. You've taken new practices and paradigms into consideration, you've reached out to someone, borrowed some words for clarification you needed in your own heart, and started adding these tools to your belt to use when needed. Any growth from the first page to here is worth celebrating. Remember, course correction only has to happen one degree at a time for us to end up where we're called to be.

Our ordinary lives are full of so many joyful moments: noticing new things on your walks and drives, texting friends because you're thinking of them, decluttering your home or your soul to make room for growth, forgiving yourself and others and setting boundaries for where you'll allow your mind to go when comparison creeps in. I can see it. I hope you can too.

Putting It into Practice

Despite the significant interruptions in life recently—like the call when my husband let me in on the fact that he'd be job hunting because things were shifting at his work, the sight of my podcasting equipment broken and scattered after my office break-in—and the subtle ones, too, I still can find joy here and know that life can be good and hard at the same time. There's no need to pick one; both can be true. But we know this frame of mind doesn't just happen, and there's no amount of willpower that can force us to think this way and take this approach. It comes with practice, discipline, and everyday habits that we all have a road map to.

Here are some ideas and quick aids when life starts life-ing for you too.

- Take a few deep breaths.
- Ground yourself by putting your bare feet on the ground outside.
- Confide in a friend. Spend intentional time with them.
- Provide order and coziness to your home by organizing that one cabinet or closet you've been putting off.
- Analyze what routines are serving you well and which ones can be tossed.
- Nourish your body and rest well.
- Make a "joy list" to refer to when you are having a hard time seeing the good.
- Go play and find ways to have fun.

The old me would have tried to perform her way through her worst days and seasons, make a list of ways she needed to improve. She would not live out of an overflowing heart, knowing grace is abundant and she could try again tomorrow.

Rachel 2.0 is doing things differently and living by the principles of this book, and believe me when I say it's better to realize that the life I love is right in front of me rather than something I have to prove and strive my way to find.

He's with Us

I'd be naive to think that just because you finished reading this book, you'd receive a badge and win an award that acts as protection from future complications of life. Those complications will still happen. They're normal, expected, and necessary parts of living the abundant life we all desire. They're not to be dismissed, wiggled out of, or sped past. We can't go around—we must go through.

As Jesus says in John 16:33, "I have said these things to you, that in me you may have peace. In the world you will have tribulation. But take heart; I have overcome the world." We will have issues, trip-ups, and setbacks—we need to expect them. But we should also expect joy and peace and abundance, because those are promised just as much.

Next time life gets tough, remember that it's necessary for your growth. If people think you're being silly when you choose to pay attention to the good things in the midst of hard times, share with them the impact this mindset has had on you. And notice who around you wants to have a part in the life you're living—and invite them in. Notice whose life you want to be a part of—and get around them.

When you start doubting the goodness of God, refer back to your joy list, recall the ways God has come through before, get honest with Him, and stop yourself from hiding from Him.

And have grace for yourself. The Lord has extended a grace that is so deep and beautiful and rich that it covers any chasm our minds and hearts create. Through it all, the greatest joy and gift that makes any life likable is the withness of God. No matter what we're going through, He's there with us in every moment.

Freely Ours

The thief comes only to steal and kill and destroy. I came that they may have life and have it abundantly.

JOHN 10:10

Have you ever noticed that breathing comes so naturally to us that, in health, we're able to do it without intentionally thinking about inhaling and exhaling? But sometimes there are moments when we must concentrate on our breathing to calm ourselves down, catch our breath, and slow our heartbeat to a gentler pace. Joy, an abundant life, and the likability of the life you're living now is, like breathing, a birthright when we belong to Jesus. It's available to us. It's freely ours.

It can become such a natural rhythm that most times we do it without thinking. Other times, it takes concentration to return to the space and pace we desire.

Joy is not a "cheer up" message, nor is it just "try and be grateful." It's most beautiful and best displayed when flaming arrows are all around but we stand with confidence, when life fractures but we still see it as beautiful, and when expectations are missed but we still call it good. That's when joy is most evident to others—but also to ourselves. Joy is made richer when we're experiencing grief because it becomes a choice and a focus rather than a natural response to something good.

Like my childhood Rollerblading adventures with my dad, we have the opportunity to live life messily and ask for help while having fun at the same time—so much so that others stop and look and want to give it a try. When we choose to focus on joy, we can't help but display it to those around us. And they'll be curious! *How can you be so joyful and content if your life isn't perfect?* Living an out-loud abundant life is one of the greatest forms of sharing Jesus with others, in my opinion. It makes this sometimes-clunky conversation so natural.

We have a few neighbors I've gotten to know over the past three years, and I adore the over-the-fence, front-yard, and roll-the-window-down-as-you-drive-past conversations. Neighbors are interesting—they see the way you live, get to know your routine, when you leave, when you get home, when your grass needs to be cut, and the wrestle to get your children buckled into car seats. There's no great hiding spot to conceal your life—the good or the hard—from the people in proximity like neighbors. My neighbors know when Thomas is gone on a work trip simply because they see him missing from our family walks and our dinner picnics on the front porch, as well as the people in and out to help me make up the slack by adding a few extra hands for kids and chores.

I'll never forget a conversation I had with one of our neighbors we're beginning to know more closely.

Thomas was deployed and had been gone for several weeks already. I was running late to an appointment, which meant I got home later than I thought I would. And that meant I missed a friend when she delivered a meal for us, knowing cooking nutritious warm meals at home was a luxury these days.

Lilly, my friend who brought the meal that night, didn't want to leave the items on our front porch. Our neighbor happened to be outside, and he began a small conversation about what she was dropping off. This neighbor offered to put the dinner she had made in his refrigerator until we got home since some of the items needed to stay cool.

"Dinner is with Mr. Pete. Love you!" Lilly texted me.

So instead of pulling into our driveway when we got home, I stopped in front of Mr. Pete's house and met him and his wife on their front porch as they sat in their rocking chairs.

"You're here for the tacos, aren't you?" He smiled and waved me inside his door as he shuffled in.

I had never been in their home or gotten to know them

past the "Oh my, the boys are getting so big" comments and waves when we passed one another in our daily routines.

But it was special. They had been in that home for years, were settled, and the peace was contagious—exactly what I needed.

"You have quite the friends to do something like this for you."

"I don't take it for granted, that's for sure."

"Remind me when Thomas comes home."

We stood in their living room for the next few minutes catching up about Thomas's deployment, our plans while he was gone, how we were holding up, and how, by God's grace, we were doing well.

Mr. Pete is a believer—we share this commonality—but we were bonded when he shared Truth with me that I needed to hear in a season I felt short of breath and I shared evidence of how joy is found through help, community, choosing a posture of hope, and chasing the fun.

Mr. Pete still gives me a nod and a wink now to say, *Hey, neighbor,* as I pretend to get knocked down when one of my boys tags me in our games in the front yard. We greet each other when I walk down the street passing out snacks to my kids, or when we happen to check the mail at the same time. Joy is contagious, available, right in front of us but easy to miss if we don't put on the right lens to see it.

We have other neighbors who witness our interactions, who know how both our lives contain some really hard situations. I've been in conversation with them, too, about how

I got to know Mr. Pete, which leads me into my "Well, he held on to some tacos for me when I was late getting home" story, which leads me into a "No, this isn't fake—I really do enjoy my life—and yes, my life is also as messy as it looks."

I can count on this typically leading into a "Hmm, why do you think that is?" question and conversation about how my hope is in something—Someone—greater.

Loving your life is whimsical, fun, trying new things, playing. It's spontaneous, creative, silly. But it's so much more than that.

And when I love my life regardless of the circumstances, and when you love your life too, those around us who don't know Jesus personally see that they, too, can have a life they love.

My brother and I were recently sharing leftovers at my counter after he helped me put the boys to bed on a night I was parenting solo—thank you, Hamilton, the best (f)uncle ever. When we were talking about this book and the way it's been pressing on my heart for the past (almost) decade, he asked me, "Hey, Ray, what's the best analogy you can think of about joy?"

I paused my chewing, thought about the answer, and finished my bite around the same time I finished my thought.

"Confetti," I answered.

Confetti is one of those vibrant, silly, celebratory things in life.

Once a confetti cannon is popped, it takes a lot of work to get rid of the evidence. It's noisy, creates commotion, instantly causes smiles, and leaves a trail signaling "Fun was had here."

Most times, it's completely unexpected.

Every little piece of confetti alone is just a scrap of paper, but together it's a whole event.

Many of us, with our confetti poppers in hand, tuck them into our pocket instead of popping them, thinking, *Maybe now's not the time.* Or perhaps we believe it's not worth the mess.

But I hope throughout this book your perspective has shifted and you've found that, in fact, the confetti of joy is always worth it—for you, and for others too. Sure, loving your life is messy because there's no way to like it *all* the time. But loving your life—and the gift of joy—is incredibly worth it.

MORE RESOURCES FOR YOU

If you are having a moment where you feel like you've tried it all and maybe you're even saying, "Rachel, these practicals won't even touch the depths of my despair or discontentment with life," I wanted to make sure there was a section like this for you.

If it's been a while since you've found joy in your life, it certainly does not disqualify you from experiencing a life you love, but it may take a different type of help to get you there. You may need to close this book right now and seek out that help before taking another piece of practical advice, implementing it, and being discouraged that, once again, you were having a hard time seeing the fruit. I want to be fair to you, your circumstances, and your mental health, which may be preventing you from crossing the chasm from not liking your life to loving it fully.

As much as I believe that, yes, this work of mine could help lead you to a life you love and give you a vision for the joyful life I want for all of us, I hope to make this clear: this is not a mental health book. This entire book would be a disservice to you if I didn't tell you that I have experienced seasons where I needed counseling, medical intervention, and unearthing of past hurts to find healing today. That kind of healing was necessary before I could seek out the joy amid the mundane details of life. I've had to get professional help, taking off the lens that dimmed life a bit to see the full and beautiful picture.

You may need that too.

If that is you, I urge you to seek out professional help. It has saved me in many seasons of my life and could be the very thing that helps pull you out too.

Also, please check out these resources to help you find healing and wholeness.

I recommend these episodes of my podcast, *Real Talk with Rachel Awtrey*:

- "Listen to This When Life Is Life'ing" with Cleere Reaves | Episode 301
- "Getting Out of a Funk" | Episode 280
- "For the Ones That 'Just Need a Break'" with Dr. Alison Cook | Episode 279
- "If You're Tired of Being Tired" with Jess Connolly | Episode 277
- "My Jaw Was on the Floor This Whole Convo" with Ellie Holcomb | Episode 272
- "Start Liking Your Life" with Sara Hagerty | Episode 265

I love these books by author friends of mine:

- *Untangle Your Emotions: Naming What You Feel and Knowing What to Do About It* by Jennie Allen
- *I Shouldn't Feel This Way: Name What's Hard, Tame Your Guilt, and Transform Self-Sabotage into Brave Action* by Dr. Alison Cook
- *Fighting Forward: Your Nitty-Gritty Guide to Beating the Lies That Hold You Back* by Hannah Brencher

With love and a lot of compassion,
Rachel Awtrey

ACKNOWLEDGMENTS

They warn authors that you'll go through what you write through, and man—that's the truth. As my cursor blinked, life started pivoting in ways that felt heavy to carry in a season that demanded inspiration and imagination. Writing a book about joy was only made possible by those who reminded me—with words, actions, and personality—that nothing in life disqualifies you from the gift of joy.

To my boys, thank you for bringing me back to my knees in prayer, for helping my sanctification process while also giving me so many cackling moments and joy-filled conversations with your precious ideas and biggest life questions. To my mom, thank you for graciously letting me tell our story. To my dad, thank you for teaching me to get back up when life knocks me down. Oh! And to both of y'all, Mom and Dad, for introducing six-year-old Rachel to what has become my "hype soundtrack" before writing days: Kirk Franklin. To my mother "in love" who prayed and covered me through this writing process and journey. The layer between heaven and earth felt so thin through this, and I honor you for that.

Emily Rowlett, my unicorn, my work wife. You corrected me when I bullied myself, and you let me cry (should we pull the doorbell camera footage?) when the calling on my life felt like too much. Thank you for making me say the scary dreams out loud.

There are a few "speed-dial" friends who are intertwined in all of these words: Abby Adams, Carla Grice, and Scarlet Stearns, your prayers and clarity when my vision was clunky and blurry picked me up and reminded me of gospel truth that I so often forget: His grace is surely sufficient for me. Oh! And also, six-thirty morning prayer meetings aren't my best look—how about we switch to evenings?

It all started with Kathleen Kerr, who believed in me, was a dream literary agent, and hopped on countless calls to celebrate and cheer me on through this process. She saw my story when I didn't see it myself.

To my editors at Tyndale: Jillian Schlossberg, you endured the random texts, toddler choking on spaghetti, bloody noses, and deep conversations, and Danika Kelly, you made it make sense. Thank you to the entire team at Tyndale that gave me the most beautiful process for my first book.

To my village in Birmingham: the fellow members of Redeemer Community Church, the Settles, my neighbors, and precious people who helped me juggle life as I fumbled through these words—it takes a village, and that entire chapter is dedicated to you. Thank you for wrangling my children; cooking me warm, nutritious meals; and helping me fold my laundry, undergarments and all.

My confidant, best friend, and husband, Thomas—your championing of me and your creativity as you pursue me always inspires the joy woven into my life. I acknowledge you, your partnership, wisdom, and eagerness to enjoy your own life as the fuel for a message like the one in these pages.

READERS' GUIDE

Introduction

1. Rachel opens the book with a story about her orchid. How do you relate to the idea of "overwatering" parts of your life instead of addressing the root problem?
2. What signs in your own life indicate you might need to step back and reevaluate your priorities?

Part 1: Unlocking Joy: The Keys You Didn't Know You Had

Chapter 1: What Is Joy? (Because the Dictionaries Got It Wrong and We May Have Too)

1. Rachel distinguishes between happiness and joy. How would you describe the difference in your own words? What does joy tell us about who God is?
2. What does joy look like in your life right now? Where do you feel it's missing?

Chapter 2: That Wasn't on My Bingo Card

1. How has joy shown up in your life during challenging or unexpected times?
2. What are some everyday moments of joy that you tend to overlook?
3. Rachel shares about life's unpredictability. What's a recent life change you've faced, and how did you adapt (or struggle to adapt)? How would the pursuit of determined joy change this for you?

Chapter 3: Breaking and Entering: When Joy Gets Jacked and How to Get It Back

1. What are the biggest joy stealers in your life (e.g., comparison, busyness, lack of boundaries)?
2. Reflect on a time when you saw God's kindness bring you back to Him after experiencing a season where joy was hard to find.

Part 2: Joy on Repeat: Building a Life You Love

Chapter 4: And 5, 6, 7, 8: Our Need for Rhythms

1. Rachel talks about creating rhythms that align with your life. What's one rhythm or habit you could implement to make your days feel more meaningful?
2. How do your current routines contribute to—or take away from—your joy?

Chapter 5: How Going Slow Made Me Steady

1. How do you currently handle the unexpected or chaotic moments in life?
2. Knowing that we've been called to return to God and rest in the freedom that Jesus gives us, how does this change the way that you rest?

Chapter 6: Joy Takes a Village—Literally

1. Who are the people in your life who help you find joy?
2. How can you foster deeper connections and joy-filled relationships with those around you?

Chapter 7: Making Fun out of the Mundane

1. How do you find joy in the ordinary or repetitive parts of life?
2. What's one mundane task you could reframe to make it feel more joyful?

Chapter 8: What Living in a Camper Taught Me

1. How can you create a home centered around gospel hospitality?
2. What typical excuses do you find and use that keep you from inviting people into your life and home?

Chapter 9: This Life Is Yours for the Taking

1. Rachel writes about finding beauty and wonder in the small things. What's one small "God-wink" moment you've experienced recently?
2. How can you intentionally look for these moments in your day-to-day life?
3. What does long-term joy look like for you?

General Reflection Questions

1. What's one insight or takeaway from *Love Your Life (Even If You Don't Like It All the Time)* that surprised you or shifted your perspective?
2. How has your understanding of joy changed after reading this book?
3. What's one action step you feel inspired to take now that you've finished this book?

NOTES

CHAPTER 4: AND 5, 6, 7, 8

1. Kendra Adachi, *The Lazy Genius Way: Embrace What Matters, Ditch What Doesn't, and Get Stuff Done* (WaterBrook, 2020), 20–35.

CHAPTER 5: HOW GOING SLOW MADE ME STEADY

1. This quote is often attributed to Corrie ten Boom.
2. Dietrich Bonhoeffer, *Psalms: The Prayer Book of the Bible* (Broadleaf Books, 2022), 15.

CHAPTER 6: JOY TAKES A VILLAGE–LITERALLY

1. Lysa TerKeurst, "In my healing journey, I often wondered how much to keep private without feeling like I was keeping secrets from my family and loved ones," Facebook, March 28, 2024, https://www.facebook.com/OfficialLysa/posts/pfbid0hoNzytnqGx85aNP5jJCchLrRVXmtVAhCWuBoSHEhmfM83X5NbjPzzHqcgFbxJ3a8l.

ABOUT THE AUTHOR

Rachel Awtrey is a trailblazing influencer and podcaster who defies conventional norms by inviting her audience to peek behind the curtain of her life. Rachel is a mom of two little boys, a military wife, and after moving nine times in her eight years of marriage, she knows a thing or two about making community wherever she is!

With an unwavering commitment to transparency, Rachel shares her personal journey, triumphs, and challenges, breaking down barriers and inspiring others to embrace their own authentic selves. Through her empowering content, she provides a unique blend of encouragement and practical tips, providing her followers with valuable tools to navigate life's obstacles with resilience and grace.

In a culture that often encourages surface-level perfection, Rachel stands out by embracing vulnerability and imperfections. Her refreshing approach creates a genuine connection with her audience, fostering a sense of community and reminding everyone that they are not alone in their struggles.

With over 1.5 million downloads of her chart-topping podcast, *Real Talk with Rachel Awtrey* (formerly *Behind the Bliss Podcast*), along with her social media platforms, Rachel is changing the game, dismantling societal expectations, and encouraging others to embrace their true selves while equipping them with valuable tools to thrive and find joy in every aspect of life.

TUNE IN TO *REAL TALK WITH RACHEL AWTREY*

Love This Book? Let's Keep the Conversation Going!

For readers of *Love Your Life (Even When You Don't Like It All the Time)*, Rachel Awtrey invites you to dive deeper into the messy, mundane, and magnificent moments of life with her podcast, *Real Talk with Rachel Awtrey*. Part of the acclaimed That Sounds Fun Network, this podcast is a heartfelt space for encouragement, practical wisdom, and unfiltered conversations about navigating life with joy and purpose.

What's *Real Talk* All About?

Real Talk with Rachel Awtrey is a space where you'll dive deeper into the questions and topics that are often avoided. Each episode is designed to encourage, inspire, and remind you that you're not alone in the places you find yourself. With relatable stories, practical tips, and unfiltered honesty, Rachel will keep unpacking what it means to find joy and live a life you love.

What You'll Hear

- **Conversations that matter:** Real talk about motherhood, faith, marriage, mental health, and personal growth.

- **Special guests:** From experts to friends, the show brings on voices that inspire and uplift. You'll hear some of your favorite women, including Ruth Chou Simons, Ellie Holcomb, Kari Jobe, Jess Connolly, Kathie Lee Gifford, and more.
- **Encouragement for the hard days:** Life is messy, but we don't have to walk through it alone.
- **Practical takeaways:** Real advice for creating rhythms, finding joy, and loving your life—even on the tough days.

Start Here! Listener Favorites

- "When Doing It All Is Undoing You" with Alyssa Bethke
- "Unplugging and Becoming More Present" with Hannah Brencher
- "Listen to This When Life is Life'ing" with Cleere Reaves

Let's Stay Connected!

- **Find *Real Talk* on Apple Podcasts, Spotify, or wherever you listen.**
- **Follow Rachel on Instagram @rachel.awtrey** for behind-the-scenes fun, podcast updates, and encouragement.

- **Share your takeaways!** Tag Rachel in your favorite moments from this book or an episode you love—let's keep the conversation going.

Life's too hard to do it alone, and *Real Talk with Rachel Awtrey* is here to remind you that you're never alone. Let's grow together, laugh together, and find joy right where we are.

Subscribe wherever you listen to podcasts today, and let's keep talking!